Problem-Solving Tools and Tips for School Leaders

Cathie E. West

Routledge
Taylor & Francis Group
New York London

First published 2011 by Eye On Education

Published 2013 by Routledge
711 Third Avenue, New York, NY 10017, USA
2 Park Square, Milton Park, Abingdon, Oxon OX14 4RN

Routledge is an imprint of the Taylor & Francis Group, an informa business

Copyright © 2011 Taylor & Francis

All rights reserved. No part of this book may be reprinted or reproduced or utilised in any form or by any electronic, mechanical, or other means, now known or hereafter invented, including photocopying and recording, or in any information storage or retrieval system, without permission in writing from the publishers.

Notices
No responsibility is assumed by the publisher for any injury and/or damage to persons or property as a matter of products liability, negligence or otherwise, or from any use of operation of any methods, products, instructions or ideas contained in the material herein.

Practitioners and researchers must always rely on their own experience and knowledge in evaluating and using any information, methods, compounds, or experiments described herein. In using such information or methods they should be mindful of their own safety and the safety of others, including parties for whom they have a professional responsibility.

Product or corporate names may be trademarks or registered trademarks, and are used only for identification and explanation without intent to infringe.

Library of Congress Cataloging-in-Publication Data

West, Cathie E.
Problem-solving tools and tips for school leaders / Cathie E. West.
p. cm.
ISBN 978-1-59667-172-0

1. Educational leadership—United States. 2. School administrators—Training of—United States. 3. Teacher-administrator relationships—United States. 4. School improvement programs—United States. I. Title.

LB2831.82.W47 2011

371.2′011—dc22

ISBN: 978-1-596-67172-0 (pbk) 2010047928

Also Available from EYE ON EDUCATION

Leading School Change:
9 Strategies to Bring *Everybody* On Board
Todd Whitaker

Get Organized! Time Management for School Leaders
Frank Buck

Classroom Walkthroughs to Improve Teaching and Learning
Donald Kachur, Judy Stout, and Claudia Edwards

The Principalship from A to Z
Ronald Williamson and Barbara R. Blackburn

Rigorous Schools and Classrooms: Leading the Way
Ronald Williamson and Barbara R. Blackburn

The Instructional Leader's Guide to Informal Classroom Observations, Second Edition
Sally J. Zepeda

Professional Learning Communities:
An Implementation Guide and Toolkit
Kathleen A. Foord and Jean M. Haar

Professional Development: What Works
Sally J. Zepeda

Motivating & Inspiring Teachers, Second Edition
Todd Whitaker, Beth Whitaker, and Dale Lumpa

Creating School Cultures that Embrace Learning: What Successful Leaders Do
Tony Thacker, John S. Bell, and Franklin P. Schargel

Executive Skills for Busy School Leaders
Chris Hitch and David Coley

Improving Your Daily Practice: A Guide for Effective School Leadership
Timothy B. Berkey

Help Teachers Engage Students:
Action Tools for Administrators
Annette Brinkman, Gary Forlini, and Ellen Williams

For John Masters West

About the Author

Cathie E. West has an MS Degree in education and more than thirty years of experience as an elementary school principal. Currently, she is the principal of a 540-student K-5 elementary school in Washington State. Cathie has been twice honored as an exemplary principal, receiving the Washington Distinguished Principal Award as the representative from Douglas County in 1998, and as the representative from Snohomish County in 2005. She also received the Leadership for Student Achievement Award from the Washington Association of School Administrators in 2009.

Cathie's professional experience includes teaching at the college level; directing special programs, such as Title I, Special Education, and Highly Capable; and coordinating curriculum and staff development for a variety of school districts. In addition, she was an Editorial Advisor for the National Association of Elementary School Principals (2002–2005) and a member of the Program Advisory Committee for the Washington State Leadership Academy (2008). Currently, Cathie serves on the editorial board for Washington State Kappan.

Cathie coauthored *Leadership Teaming: The Superintendent-Principal Relationship* (Corwin Press, 2009) with Dr. Mary Lynne Derrington. Her writing has appeared in The *Principal News* (AWSP), *Washington State Kappan* (PDK), *Principal* (NAESP), *Communicator* (NAESP), and *ERS Spectrum*. Cathie can be reached at cathiewest@comcast.net.

Acknowledgements

This book is the product of a long and rewarding professional journey that has included countless opportunities to learn from others—talented teachers, dedicated program directors, powerful principals, and sterling superintendents. My appreciation for these phenomenal educators runs wide and deep.

I am also indebted to Bob Sickles, the superb editor of Eye On Education for his astute guidance, insightful suggestions, and unfailing support throughout the developmental stages of this book and during the production process.

I extend my appreciation to the discerning reviewers of my book as it was being drafted and to the members of the editorial and production departments at Eye On Education for helping me craft a book I can share with confidence.

Free Downloads

Many of the tools discussed and displayed in this book are also available on the Routledge website as Adobe Acrobat files. Permission has been granted to purchasers of this book to download these tools and print them.

You can access these downloads by visiting www.routledge.com/9781596671720 and click on the Free Downloads tab.

List of Free Downloads

Figure 1.1 Staff Interview Questions....page 3
Figure 1.2 School Facility & Grounds Checklist....page 5
Figure 1.3 School Systems and Services Survey....page 9
Figure 2.2 My First Job....page 39
Figure 2.3 Teacher Q & A....page 40
Figure 2.5 Center 5: Science Instruction Input....page 45
Figure 2.6 Center 10: Principal's Mission....page 46
Figure 2.7 Teacher Goal Plan....page 48
Figure 3.3 Staff Code of Conduct....page 64
Figure 4.1 Threatening Intruder Response Plan....page 89
Figure 5.1 Theory of Action Staff Meeting....page 108
Figure 5.10 Staff Meeting: School Improvement Plan....page 129
Figure 5.11 Staff Meeting: Math Assessments....page 130
Figure 5.12 Staff Meeting: Writing Evaluation....page 131
Figure 6.3 Principal Daily Checklist....page 151
Figure 6.5 Staff Development Guide....page 159

Contents

About the Author vii
Acknowledgements ix
Free Downloads xi
Introduction xvii
- Special Features xvii
- Concept and Skill Exploration xviii
- Who This Book Is For xviii
- Why I Wrote This Book xviii
- What You Will Learn xix

Theme 1 Perfecting Problem-Solving Performance 1
- Talk to People in the Know 2
- Survey the Scene 4
- Take Stock 7
  - Suggested Readings 19
- Triage Your Troubles 19
  - Suggested Readings 21
- Step Up to Problem Solving 22
- Empower Potential Problem Solvers 27
  - Suggested Reading 29
- Summing Up 29
- Making Connections 30
- Strengthening Professional Practice 30

Theme 2 Counteracting Workplace Negativity 31
- Cultivate Constructive Actions 32
  - Suggested Readings 33
- Affirm 33
- Showcase Relationship Role Models 37
- Be Efficient 41
- Orchestrate 47
- Put Out Fires 49
  - Suggested Readings 50
- Summing Up 50
- Making Connections 50
- Strengthening Professional Practice 50

Theme 3 Stopping Staff Misconduct 53
Spell It Out 54
Create Conduct Norms 63
Provide Field Trip Guidelines 65
Teach 69
Intervene 74
Suggested Readings 77
Send for the Cavalry 77
Suggested Readings 82
Summing Up 82
Making Connections 82
Strengthening Professional Practice 83

Theme 4 Mastering Emergency Management 85
Take Charge 86
Suggested Readings 87
Simplify 88
Use Protocols 91
Activate a Support Team 92
Practice, Practice, Practice 96
Set Student Expectations 100
Summing Up 102
Making Connections 103
Strengthening Professional Practice 103

Theme 5 Breaking Through Success Barriers 105
Develop a Theory of Action 106
Keep Tinkering 109
Craft Master Plans 115
Disaggregate Data 117
Suggested Readings 124
Power-up Staff Meetings 124
Engineer Sustainability 132
Suggested Reading 134
Summing Up 134
Making Connections 135
Strengthening Professional Practice 135

Theme 6 Derailing Leadership Distress 137
Craft Stress Response Plans 138
Suggested Reading 141
Stay Healthy 141
Suggested Reading 143

Set Realistic Goals 143
Stay on Top of Your Workload 149
Keep Organized 154
Suggested Readings 157
Perfect Performance 157
Suggested Readings 160
Summing Up 160
Making Connections 161
Strengthening Professional Practice 161

Conclusion 163
Additional Suggested Readings 165
References 167

Introduction

School leadership has substantial rewards but it is not without a few problems. The day-to-day operation of a school brings countless irritants: scheduling conflicts, plumbing disasters, staff no-shows, late buses, and the like. A second layer of trouble springs from the formidable responsibilities associated with serving as an instructional leader. This extraordinary job includes updating curriculum, initiating new teaching practices, overseeing the implementation of instructional programs, supervising and evaluating teachers, and meeting state and federal accountability mandates. To complicate matters, health and safety emergencies suddenly arise threatening the wellbeing of students or staff or both. In a heartbeat this kind of trouble trumps all others becoming the school leader's number one problem-solving priority. Sound overwhelming? Not for school leaders who are proactive and well prepared. These savvy administrators have a toolkit full of highly effective problem-solving—and problem preventing—strategies. You will find these strategies in *Problem-Solving Tools and Tips for School Leaders.*

Special Features

This problem-solving guide presents a wide range of leadership challenges organized under the following themes:

- Perfecting Problem-Solving Performance
- Counteracting Workplace Negativity
- Stopping Staff Misconduct
- Mastering Emergency Management
- Breaking Through Success Barriers
- Derailing Leadership Distress

Each theme is supported by a variety of problem-solving tips that are accompanied by authentic stories, practical examples, and ready-to-use tools. *Problem-Solving Tools and Tips for School Leaders* also serves as a sourcebook for related professional resources—books, journals, websites, and online references.

Concept and Skill Exploration

To help readers review, apply, and retain new learning, these helpful features appear at the close of each theme:

- ♦ Summing Up

  Provides a bulleted summary of each theme's major concepts to help you review and retain new concepts and strategies.
- ♦ Making Connections

  Lists thought-provoking reflection questions—ideal for individual or group book studies.
- ♦ Strengthening Professional Practice

  Suggests practical activities that help you apply the concepts and skills you have learned.

Who This Book Is For

This book is directed primarily at principals but the audience also includes vice-principals, administrative interns, program directors, teacher leaders, and other educators in leadership roles. This book teaches readers how to confidently prepare for and respond to a variety of schoolhouse problems—from pesky to crisis level. There are ideas that can be put to work exactly as described, as well as suggestions and resources that can be adapted to fit the unique situations school leaders encounter in their schools.

Why I Wrote This Book

At the start of my principal career I confronted a succession of perplexing problems but had no guide, such as a mentor or coach, to help me find solutions. I was hesitant to go to my superintendent for suggestions, although I admired him immensely. My exceptional boss was overtaxed from the demands of running our large, ever-expanding school district, and besides, I was reluctant to admit that I didn't know what to do.

On occasion I worked up the courage to ask the superintendent's busy assistant for advice, but this veteran administrator thought I knew more than I did. He issued cryptic directives I found bewildering—like the time I called to report that one of my aides had broken a window in anger. The assistant told me to fire the errant employee on the spot then abruptly hung up to take a more urgent call. I had never fired anyone before and had *no* idea how to go about this breath taking assignment.

To this day it amazes me that I was left to puzzle out employee dismissal procedures on my own.

Fortunately, I soon learned that when problems arose I could rely on the expertise and good will of the more experienced school leaders all around me. I began contacting principals, program directors, and even my own teachers for advice, and these generous souls never failed me. Now, after several decades as a successful school principal, it is time to pay back. I wrote *Problem-Solving Tools and Tips for School Leaders* to help others—teacher leaders striving to expand their skills, brand new administrators looking for guidance, and experienced principals confronting new problems or looking for fresh problem-solving ideas.

What You Will Learn

This book presents concepts and strategies derived from in-depth professional experience—more than thirty years as a successful school principal; powerful insights gained from experiencing startling successes and memorable failures; and the wisdom accrued from fortuitous associations with an abundance of bright, creative, and resourceful school leaders. The information presented also reflects extensive research, such as interviews with noteworthy educators and a review of the contemporary literature on "best practices" in education, business, sociology, and psychology.

Problem-Solving Tools and Tips for School Leaders will teach you that trouble and trying times are inevitable; that problems provide opportunities to stimulate your thinking, test your resourcefulness, and fine-tune your leadership skills; and that maintaining an optimistic attitude and a "can do" spirit are as important as the quality of the problem-solving strategies employed.

Can all problems be fixed? Of course not! But those that can will bring the satisfaction that comes from a job well done and those that cannot will offer the chance to manage them so effectively their impact upon the people you serve becomes negligible. With this in mind, I hope *Problem-Solving Tools and Tips for School Leaders* helps you solve the thorny problems you face and keeps you from having to puzzle things out on your own.

Theme 1

Perfecting Problem-Solving Performance

I love the man that can smile in trouble, that can gather strength from distress and grow brave by reflection.

— Thomas Paine (1776)

The town I live and work in was fortunate to receive a grant for a highway that would reroute large trucks away from the city core. Although construction of the new route would run directly behind my school—causing the din, dust, and delays associated with such projects—I was delighted as pedestrian and vehicular safety would be vastly improved. I was startled, however, to be notified shortly after the project began that a boundary line glitch placed several of my portable classrooms in the path of the road work. Even though school was in full swing and these portables fully occupied, they would have to be moved and the students they housed crammed into the main building of my overcrowded school. What was the timeline for the move? Immediately! This alarming development was another reminder that there is no shortage of trouble for a school principal.

When trouble strikes school leaders must do more than endure. Successful school leaders tackle problems quickly, intentionally, optimistically, and proficiently. As importantly, they help their teachers and support staffs handle problems constructively and grow from setbacks. These magical leaders are also proactive. They look for ways to *prevent* problems or at the very least, address them in the early stages before they grow to crisis proportions.

Theme 1 explores the problem-solving concepts and skills that are used by these savvy school leaders and provides practical suggestions for improving problem-preventing and problem-solving performances. You will learn techniques for identifying and prioritizing the troubles you encounter, tackling problems systematically, and implementing a variety of problem-solving procedures. Whether you find brand new strategies to employ or come across tips you have forgotten to put to work, be assured that *each* strategy is designed to make your problem-solving pursuits rewarding ones.

Talk to People in the Know

It has been said that one picture is worth a thousand words but I learned early on that one interview—with a person in the know—can paint a thousand pictures. I discovered the power of interviews when I was a young girl on a cross-country road trip with my parents. My mother had given me a packet of No. 2 pencils and several spiral-bound notebooks to keep me occupied and I used these journalistic tools to record information about the people I encountered along the way. Not celebrities or dignitaries, but ordinary folks like park rangers, gas station mechanics, and grocery store clerks.

Although a novice newshound, I ferreted out an amazing amount of information. I learned from an inn keeper, for example, that his job was a mixed bag of responsibilities—registering guests, keeping the inn's books, supervising a platoon of employees, hauling trash, and folding laundry. Despite working 24/7, he loved serving people and the variety his job offered. The observations of this enterprising business man—and the other "ordinary" folks I interviewed—were eye opening.

Decades later when I assumed the leadership of a large elementary school, I begin learning about my school *not* by reading its performance reports, improvement plans, and handbooks but by interviewing the people who were "in the know." One by one I talked to teachers, specialists, secretaries, cooks, custodians, aides, and food service workers. After quizzing the interviewees about their personal interests and job responsibilities, I asked the questions shown in Figure 1.1.

The staff members, I discovered, were highly dedicated and valued the children and families they served. Nevertheless, pockets of problems were revealed—the students were cooperative but coasting academically; the teachers were experienced and well educated but not working as a team; the classified staff was enthusiastic but felt unappreciated; and the previous principal had been competent but a shade "too nice." Many staff members believed he had been reluctant to confront problems, such as the students' academic decline and the lack of teamwork among the teachers. The interviews gave me the details I needed to begin my leadership work but, as importantly, helped me connect with my new staff. Listening to and learning from your people is a vital relationship building endeavor (Dolan, 1994).

How can interviews work for you? Whether you are new to your school, or have been there a while, paint a picture of your school's strengths

Figure 1.1 Staff Interview Questions

Staff Member: ____________________ Assignment: _________________

Tell me about yourself—your life outside school, family, and interests.

____

____

____

____

Describe your education, training, and work experiences.

____

____

____

____

Tell me about your work—your assignment and responsibilities.

____

____

____

____

What is going well here?

____

____

____

____

Do you think anything needs fine-tuning?

____

____

____

____

Are there any suggestions that you have for me?

____

____

____

____

strengths—and problems—through personal interviews. All you need is a No. 2 pencil, a spiral-bound notebook, and individual talking time with your own "people in the know."

Survey the Scene

When I was gearing up for my first school camp adventure, I called upon Max for pointers. Max was a retired principal who had considerable experience running outdoor education programs. Max began my training by taking me to the school's rustic camp grounds hidden high up in the mountains several hours away from our community. I hated to carve out time for this visit and tried to convince Max to skip it. But Max insisted that we could not open camp without a visit to its facilities and grounds to "survey the scene."

Once we toured the camp site, I knew how right Max had been. We had encountered a cabin whose roof had collapsed from the weight of winter snow, an impressive rodent infestation in the main lodge, a mammoth tree that had fallen across a major hiking trail, and burst water pipes in the latrines. There was also a significant amount of snow covering the ground and given the late winter weather we'd been experiencing, it was unlikely it would melt before camp began. Each of these discoveries required immediate followup if we were to open and run camp successfully. As we made a checklist of things "to do," I was thankful that Max had taken me to "survey the scene."

Back at school I reflected upon what I had learned and began to walk about my school with a more discerning eye. I noticed conditions I might have overlooked in the past, such as partially blocked hallway exits, broken tiles that had become trip hazards, missing evacuation maps, and dangerously cluttered storage closets. Eventually I crafted a checklist (Figure 1.2) that I keep on the clipboard that I carry when I am out and about in my school. I quickly jot down a problem on the checklist and pass it on to my custodian who handles it himself or refers the problem to the district's maintenance director.

Taking time to "survey the scene" will help you identify problems that might go unnoticed and lead to corrective actions that will enhance your school's functionality, safety, and attractiveness. So the next time you tour your school, keep your eyes open and a checklist handy.

(Text continues on page 7.)

Figure 1.2 School Facility & Grounds Checklist

Location	Problem	Request	Completion Date
Front of School ☐ Flag Pole ☐ Entrance Way ☐ Sidewalks ☐ Lawn/Shrubs/Trees ☐ Curbs/Gutters ☐ Parking Lot ☐ Reader Board			
Foyer ☐ Flooring ☐ Doors ☐ Window Glass			
Office Area ☐ Flooring ☐ Offices ☐ Conference Room ☐ Restrooms ☐ Workroom ☐ Staff Room			
Hallways & Restrooms ☐ A Wing ☐ B Wing ☐ C Wing ☐ D Hallway ☐ Office Hallway			

(Figure continues on next page.)

Location	Problem	Request	Completion Date
Teaching Areas ☐ Classrooms ☐ Library ☐ Music Room ☐ Gym			
Food Service ☐ Kitchen ☐ Freezer/Cooler ☐ Food Prep Equipment			
Storage Areas ☐ A Wing ☐ B Wing ☐ C Wing ☐ D Hallway ☐ Office Hallway ☐ Gym			
Back of School ☐ Fencing ☐ Lawn Areas ☐ Walking Path			
Playground Area ☐ Play Equipment ☐ Black Top ☐ Fields ☐ Fencing & Gates			

Location	Problem	Request	Completion Date
Major Systems ☐ Alarm ☐ Electric/Gas ☐ Heating/Cooling ☐ Water/Plumbing ☐ Lighting			
Other ______________ ______________ ______________ ______________ ______________ ______________ ______________			

Take Stock

Awhile back I lost half of my school. No, it wasn't carelessness on my part—the elementary schools in my district were reconfigured and my K–3 grade school was transformed, after many months of work, into a K–5. Half of my primary students and teachers went to a nearby intermediate school in exchange for half of this school's students and teachers. This propitious change dramatically altered the people and programs in my school.

When the switch occurred I didn't worry about working with the incoming fourth and fifth grade students. I had prior experience with this grade range and had known these same children as primary students. What *did* concern me were a variety of *very* complex and *very* demanding restructuring tasks that included successfully integrating the incoming intermediate teachers into their new school culture, blending the primary and intermediate faculties into a cohesive whole, developing an intermediate curriculum that complemented the primary program, and smoothly implementing the many changes we had made to our school schedule and services. Fortunately, my newly reconfigured staff approached these hurdles positively and professionally and after just a few months, our K–5 program appeared to be an unqualified success. But was it?

A principal's perception is rarely accurate as the hectic nature of leading a school makes it easy to miss small but significant problems. So what looks good on the surface might in fact be flawed and bring trouble later. So I decided to take stock of our new K–5 experience.

To accomplish this task, I fell back on a tried-and-true method for quickly finding out what is really going on. I used a detailed questionnaire (Figure 1.3) to learn about the instructional staffs' satisfaction with school communications, schedules, major events, and programs and services. Included were questions about teachers' professional development interests and *my* services because I wanted to make sure needs were being met. The survey was anonymous so that it would appeal to staff members who are reluctant to share views openly.

Surveys need not be complicated but there *is* a certain degree of planning involved. You need to choose your survey respondents; decide which questions to ask; select a response mode, such as open-ended questions or a rating scale; and the survey means—e-mail, printed, or web based. Once you have collected the completed surveys, you also need to record and analyze the responses (Thomas, 2004). My questionnaire was completed by twenty-nine certificated staff members and I took time with the data—each response was carefully coded, recorded, and analyzed. Numerical totals were also provided for the various survey categories so that comparisons could be made. Figures 1.4 (page 15) and 1.5 (page 18) are examples of how to display the type of data I collected.

The survey results told me that leadership and communication were strong and that a couple of programs, Title I and Special Education, were well regarded. But there were also trouble spots, such as a program for advanced learners that needed fine-tuning, schedules that were out of sync, and a fair amount of dissatisfaction with teacher-directed grade-level meetings. Although we had more work to do, knowing *where* to start was reassuring.

The anonymous questionnaire gave staff members the chance to share their views in a risk-free manner. Their responses identified school strengths but also problems that required attention. Are surveys a part of your troubleshooting tool kit? They ought to be.

(Text continues on page 19.)

Figure 1.3 School Systems and Services Survey

PURPOSE

Your views and ideas are needed to improve our school! Please complete the rating scales in this questionnaire and add comments and suggestions that will help me understand your thinking. Thank you.

COMMUNICATION

(1) Check (√) the communications you read and identify the frequency:

			Always	Sometimes	Seldom
a.	___	E-Mail Weekly Bulletin	☐	☐	☐
b.	___	E-Mail News Breaks	☐	☐	☐
c.	___	Mailbox Notices	☐	☐	☐
d.	___	Tiger Tales Newsletter	☐	☐	☐
e.	___	Parent Monthly Calendar/ Bulletin	☐	☐	☐
f.	___	Principal Advisory Council Minutes	☐	☐	☐
g.	___	Board Reports	☐	☐	☐
h.	___	Budget Updates	☐	☐	☐

(2) Check (√) the parts of the Weekly Bulletin that you find helpful or of interest:

a.	___	This Week's Main Events	f.	___	Due
b.	___	It's Your Turn	g.	___	Research Tidbits
c.	___	Child Study Team Meetings	h.	___	Article and Book Excerpts
d.	___	Upcoming Events	i.	___	Quips & Quotes
e.	___	General News	j.	___	Birthdays

		Excellent	Good	Satisfactory	Poor
k.	Rate the quality of the Weekly Bulletin:	☐	☐	☐	☐

l. Suggestions/Comments:

(Figure continues on next page.)

SCHEDULES

(3) The major schedules that govern our operations are listed below. For each schedule, identify the level of your satisfaction using the rating scale provided.

		Does Not Apply	Very Satisfied	Somewhat Satisfied	Not Satisfied
a.	Daily Schedule: Recess, Lunch, etc.	☐	☐	☐	☐
b.	Specialist Schedule	☐	☐	☐	☐
c.	Reading Block Schedule	☐	☐	☐	☐
d.	P-T Conference Schedule	☐	☐	☐	☐
e.	Title I Schedule	☐	☐	☐	☐
f.	Special Education Schedule	☐	☐	☐	☐
g.	Computer Lab Schedule	☐	☐	☐	☐
h.	Suggestions/Comments:				

MAJOR EVENTS

(4) The major activities for the first half of the school year are listed below. For each activity, identify the level of your satisfaction using the rating scale provided:

		Did Not Attend	Very Satisfied	Somewhat Satisfied	Not Satisfied
a.	Gr. K-5 Open House	☐	☐	☐	☐
b.	Gr. 1-5 Student Orientation Assembly	☐	☐	☐	☐
c.	Gr. K-5 Veteran's Day Assembly	☐	☐	☐	☐

		Did Not Attend	Very Satisfied	Somewhat Satisfied	Not Satisfied
d.	Parent-Teacher Conferences	☐	☐	☐	☐
e.	Staff & Student P.J. Day	☐	☐	☐	☐
f.	Student Photos	☐	☐	☐	☐
g.	Student Council Election	☐	☐	☐	☐
h.	Principal-Directed Staff Meetings (e.g. Aug. Center Mtg, Code of Collaboration Skits, Emergency Handbook Exercise, Math Measurement Mtg)	☐	☐	☐	☐
i.	Teacher-Directed Grade Level Meetings	☐	☐	☐	☐
j.	Suggestions/Comments:				

PROGRAMS & SERVICES

(5) The major services provided for students and/or teachers are listed below. For each service, identify the level of your satisfaction using the rating scale provided:

		Need More Information	Very Satisfied	Somewhat Satisfied	Not Satisfied
a.	Front Office Services	☐	☐	☐	☐

(Figure continues on next page.)

		Need More Information	Very Satisfied	Somewhat Satisfied	Not Satisfied
b.	Student Health Services	☐	☐	☐	☐
c.	Student Study Team	☐	☐	☐	☐
d.	Child Study Team	☐	☐	☐	☐
e.	Tech Support	☐	☐	☐	☐
f.	Student Discipline Support	☐	☐	☐	☐
g.	Custodial Services	☐	☐	☐	☐

(6) The major programs serving "remedial" and "accelerated" students are listed below. For each program, identify how effectively the program meets the needs of students.

		Need More Information	Very Effective	Somewhat Effective	Not Effective
a.	Title I Reading & Math	☐	☐	☐	☐
b.	Special Education	☐	☐	☐	☐
c.	Washington Reading Corp	☐	☐	☐	☐
d.	Counseling (e.g. Groups, Classes, Beh. Plans)	☐	☐	☐	☐
e.	Multi-age	☐	☐	☐	☐
f.	Challenge/H-Cap	☐	☐	☐	☐
g.	Suggestions/Comments:				

CURRICULUM & INSTRUCTION

(7) What help do *you* need to be a more effective teacher in the subject areas listed below?

a. Reading ______________________________
____

b. Math ______________________________
____

c. Writing ______________________________
____

d. Science ______________________________
____

PRINCIPAL

8. Some responsibilities of the principal are listed below. For each responsibility, rate the principal's effectiveness using the rating scale provided.

	Need More Information	Very Effective	Somewhat Effective	Not Effective
a. Managing change	☐	☐	☐	☐
b. Contributing to a positive culture	☐	☐	☐	☐
c. Listening & communicating	☐	☐	☐	☐
d. Contributing to staff professional growth	☐	☐	☐	☐
e. Setting high standards	☐	☐	☐	☐
f. Organizing & facilitating meetings	☐	☐	☐	☐
g. Being productive	☐	☐	☐	☐
h. Keeping visible	☐	☐	☐	☐

(Figure continues on next page.)

		Need More Information	Very Effective	Somewhat Effective	Not Effective
i.	Supporting staff	☐	☐	☐	☐
j.	Supporting students	☐	☐	☐	☐
k.	Working with parents	☐	☐	☐	☐
l.	Organizing school operations	☐	☐	☐	☐
m.	Overseeing the school budget	☐	☐	☐	☐
n.	Comments/Suggestions:				

STAFF MEMBER CHARACTERISTICS

(9) Check (√) the characteristics that apply to you:

a.	___	Classroom Teacher	d.	___	I serve primary students (Gr. K-3)
b.	___	Specialist	e.	___	I serve intermediate students (Gr. 4-5)
c.	___	Other	f.	___	I serve primary & intermediate students (Gr. K-5)

PLEASE...RETURN TO _______'s MAIL BOX

Figure 1.4 Survey Data Display: Question 2

Question 2 Systems and Services Survey

Question 2: Check (√) the parts of the Weekly Bulletin you find helpful or of interest. Rate the quality of the Weekly Bulletin.

	a.	b.	c.	d.	e.	f.	g.
ID	This Week	Your Turn	Mtg. Dates	Events	News	Due	Research
1	1	1	1	1	1	1	0
2	1	0	1	1	1	1	0
3	1	1	1	1	1	1	1
4	1	1	0	1	1	1	0
5	1	0	1	1	0	1	0
6	1	1	1	1	1	1	1
7	1	1	0	1	1	1	1
8	1	1	0	1	1	1	1
9	1	0	0	1	1	1	1
10	1	1	1	1	1	1	1
11	1	1	1	1	1	1	1
12	1	1	1	1	1	1	0
13	0	0	0	1	0	1	0
14	1	1	1	1	1	1	0
15	1	1	1	1	0	0	0
16	1	1	1	1	1	1	1
17	1	1	1	1	1	1	0
18	1	1	0	1	1	1	1
19	1	1	1	1	0	1	0
20	0	0	1	1	1	1	1
21	1	1	1	1	1	1	1
22	1	1	1	1	1	1	1
23	1	1	1	1	1	1	1
24	1	1	0	1	1	1	0
25	1	1	0	1	1	1	0

(Figure continues on next page.)

ID	a. This Week	b. Your Turn	c. Mtg. Dates	d. Events	e. News	f. Due	g. Research
26	1	1	1	1	1	0	1
27	1	1	1	1	1	1	1
28	1	1	1	1	1	1	1
29	1	0	0	1	1	0	0
NO.	**27**	**23**	**20**	**29**	**25**	**26**	**16**
%	**93%**	**79%**	**69%**	**100%**	**86%**	**90%**	**55%**

Code: 1 = Yes; 0 = No; NO. # YES Responses; % = Percent YES Responses

	h.	i.	j.	k. Quality			
ID	**Excerpts**	**Quips**	**Birthdays**	**Excellent**	**Good**	**Satisfactory**	**Poor**
1	0	0	0	0	1	0	0
2	0	0	1	1	0	0	0
3	1	1	1	1	0	0	0
4	0	0	0	1	0	0	0
5	0	0	0	0	1	0	0
6	0	1	0	0	0	0	0
7	0	0	1	1	0	0	0
8	0	0	0	1	0	0	0
9	1	1	0	0	1	0	0
10	1	0	1	1	0	0	0
11	1	1	1	1	0	0	0
12	0	0	0	1	0	0	0
13	0	0	0	0	1	0	0
14	0	0	1	1	0	0	0
15	0	0	1	0	1	0	0
16	1	1	1	1	0	0	0
17	0	0	1	1	0	0	0
18	1	1	1	1	0	0	0
19	0	0	1	1	0	0	0
20	0	1	0	1	0	0	0
21	1	1	1	1	0	0	0

	h.	i.	j.	k. Quality			
ID	Excerpts	Quips	Birthdays	Excellent	Good	Satisfactory	Poor
22	1	1	1	1	0	0	0
23	1	1	1	1	0	0	0
24	0	0	0	1	0	0	0
25	1	1	1	1	0	0	0
26	0	1	1	1	0	0	0
27	1	1	1	1	0	0	0
28	1	1	1	1	0	0	0
29	0	0	1	1	0	0	0
NO.	**12**	**14**	**19**	**23**	**5**	**0**	**0**
%	**41%**	**48%**	**66%**	**79%**	**17%**	**0%**	**0%**

Code: 1 = Yes; 0 = No; NO. # YES Responses; % = Percent YES Responses

Figure 1.5 Survey Data Display: Question 5

Question 5 Systems and Services Survey

Question 5: The major services provided for students and/or teachers are listed below. For each service, identify the level of your satisfaction using the rating scale provided:

	a.	b.	c.	d.	e.	f.	g.
ID	Office	Health	SST	CST	Tech	Discipline	Custodial
1	3	3	2	1	2	3	2
2	3	3	3	0	3	0	3
3	3	3	3	3	3	3	3
4	3	3	2	2	2	2	3
5	3	3	3	3	3	2	3
6	3	3	0X	0X	2	3	3
7	3	3	3	3	3	3	3
8	3	3	0X	2	2	2	3
9	1	3	0X	0X	2	3	3
10	3	3	3	3	3	2	3
11	3	3	2	2	3	3	3
12	2	2	2	3	2	2	3
13	3	3	0	0	2	3	3
14	3	2	3	3	2	3	3
15	3	3	3	3	3	3	3
16	3	3	3	3	2	3	3
17	3	3	3	3	3	3	3
18	3	3	3	2	0X	3	3
19	3	3	3	3	2	3	3
20	3	3	2	2	1	1	3
21	3	3	3	3	2	2	3
22	3	3	0X	2	1	2	3
23	3	3	3	3	0	3	3
24	3	3	0	0	2	3	3
25	3	3	0	0	3	0	3
26	3	3	3	3	3	3	3

	a.	b.	c.	d.	e.	f.	g.
ID	Office	Health	SST	CST	Tech	Discipline	Custodial
27	3	3	3	3	3	3	3
28	3	3	3	3	3	3	3
29	3	3	0	0	1	3	3
Total	**84/87**	**85/87**	**58/87**	**58/87**	**61/87**	**72/87**	**86/87**
Mean	**2.9**	**2.93**	**2**	**2**	**2.1**	**2.5**	**2.97**

0 = Incomplete Response; 0X = Respondent Needs More Information; 1 = Not Satisfied; 2 = Somewhat Satisfied; 3 = Very Satisfied; ***Note:*** Total Possible Points: 87

Suggested Readings

Bernhardt, Victoria L., & Geise, Bradley J. (2009). *From questions to actions: Using questionnaire data for continuous school improvement.* Larchmont, NY: Eye On Education.

Thomas, Susan J. (2004). *Using web and paper questionnaires for data-based decision-making: From design to interpretation of results.* Thousand Oaks, CA: Corwin Press.

Triage Your Troubles

Some principals think they need to be superheroes to keep up with the troubles that accompany school life. Problems fly at school leaders from so many sources: federal, state, and county governments and agencies; state departments of education; district-level administrators; and students, staff, and parents. Trouble even descends upon principals from "acts of God" such as adverse weather conditions that threaten the safe operation of school.

How does bad news arrive? Usually through personal contacts, such as visits with parents or meetings with staff members. Trouble also comes by way of electronic mail, snail mail, and phone communications—calls, faxes, voice mail, and text messages. There are even times when bad news is actually delivered by a messenger—a subpoena to appear in court, for example. Problems also emerge from the activities of the principal, such as employee observations, facility walkthroughs, program surveys, and data analysis. What types of trouble do school leaders encounter? Here are a few examples:

Sources	Means	Problems
State Department of Education	E-mail	(A) Your school's Accelerated Learner Program has identified too many students—the student roster has to be trimmed by 20% or state funding will be withheld.
Community Health Department	Certified Mail	(B) During a recent inspection mold was found in a crawl space over a classroom. The mold has to be removed immediately or the classroom will have to be vacated.
Superintendent	Phone Call	(C) Because of an unexpected districtwide enrollment shortfall, your school's budget has been reduced by 10%. The orders your teachers placed for teaching materials, however, have increased by 10%. Ordering priorities need to be established.
District Program Director	Text Message	(D) Your remedial reading program no longer qualifies for grant funds and your Reading Specialist must be transferred to another school. You need to determine how classroom teachers will handle students who are struggling in reading.
Principal	Data Analysis	(E) A look at interim test results for science reveals that students in the classrooms of inexperienced teachers have lower scores than students in the classrooms of veterans. The inexperienced teachers need expert help.
Staff	Personal Contact	(F) You learn from your secretary that a teacher ridiculed a student in the front hallway. You must speak to the teacher ASAP.
Student	Principal Observation	(G) You observe a student in a fifth grade class being noncompliant and disrespectful toward a substitute teacher. An intervention is required.
Parent	Voice Mail	(H) A parent notifies you that her first grader is being teased and called names on the bus. The parent demands that the bullying be stopped immediately.

When you are up to your eyeballs in problems how do you cope? The key is to establish problem-solving priorities and to do it quickly. When disaster strikes, rescue workers prioritize *their* interventions by using a "triage" system. Triage is the "sorting and allocation of treatment to…disaster victims according to a system…designed to maximize the number of survivors" (Merriam-Webster's, 2008, p. 1334). This same approach is used in the business world to funnel resources to projects that have the most chance of succeeding. I use the triage concept to sort school problems into three priority levels: Level I: Health and Safety—these concerns *always* come first; Level 2: Student Welfare; and Level 3: School Operation and Mission. Some examples for each level are listed below.

Priority	Concerns	Problems
Level 1	Health and Safety	(B) Mold in Crawl Space
Level 2	Student Welfare	(D) Service to Struggling Readers (F) Student Ridicule (H) Student Bullying
Level 3	School Operation and Mission	(A) Accelerated Learner Program (C) Ordering Priorities (E) Low Science Scores (G) Student Disrespect

Within each category I prioritize problems after considering the *urgency* and the *impact* of the concern. To give examples, in the third category (School Operation and Mission), I identified Problem G as *urgent* because I needed to stop the mistreatment of the substitute teacher and prevent classmates from mimicking the student's disrespect. I tackled the Accelerated Learner issue, Problem A, next because of the seriousness of the *impact*—losing state funding. Problem E, the poor science scores, followed because the inexperienced teachers' inadequate teaching was negatively impacting students. Dead last on my priority list was Problem C, the ordering conundrum, because there was *no* urgency or immediate impact.

I don't have to be Wonder Woman to tackle all the problems that come my way. I stay on top of problems—and keep my sanity—by prioritizing my interventions. So when you are overwhelmed with trouble—triage.

Suggested Readings

Isaacson, Leanna Stohr. (2005). *Smart, fast, efficient: The new principals guide to success*. Larchmont, NY: Eye On Education.

McEwan, Elaine K. (2003). *10 Traits of highly effective principals: From good to great performance*. Thousand Oaks, CA: Corwin Press.

Step Up to Problem Solving

In their illuminating book *Building Smart Teams: A Roadmap to High Performance* (2004), Beatty and Scott observe that most problem-solving protocols share the same steps: "…problem identification and description, problem analysis, option generation, solution selection, action planning, and follow through" (p. 40). Beatty and Scott kick problem-solving protocols up a notch, however, by emphasizing the importance of a *team* response and adding these vital ingredients: collaboration, open and thorough communication, and divergent thinking.

I got the chance to explore the authors' ideas early one morning when a school bus leaked a copious amount of diesel fuel across my school's large asphalt parking area. The spill made the area, which did double duty as a playground, completely unusable. To compound matters, toxic fumes began to waft slowly but steadily into the school. I quickly consulted "hazardous spills" in my *School Emergency Guide* and found just a couple of short paragraphs on the subject, none of which were specific enough to help me with my situation. The guide's *Principal Emergency Checklist* (Figure 1.6, pages 24–26), did give me some important crisis management steps, such as notifying the superintendent and staff about the emergency, but did not address diesel spills. What to do? Then I remembered Beatty and Scott's team emphasis and got on the phone. I soon had a cadre of experts—police, fire department, school district facility and grounds personnel—to assist me.

Getting help was critical because the diesel spill quickly grew in scope and significance. In addition to doing something about the fuel on the school grounds, for example, my "To Do" list now included doing something about the fuel that had dribbled across the streets and crosswalks leading to the school, arranging for indoor recesses for our large student body, finding a way to deliver food needed for lunch, determining how to get buses to the school at dismissal times, arranging for children who walked to be picked up as the pathways from school were contaminated, and keeping anxious parents—and their vehicles—out of the area. This latter concern complicated matters as a large number of students—about 100—were picked up at the end of the school day.

Remarkably, solutions were found for *every* problem. Some came quickly, such as shutting down the ventilation system to prevent fumes from entering the school, but other solutions took time. There was specialized information to be shared, options to be generated, and the "pros" and "cons" of various solutions debated.

My team worked collaboratively, communicated fearlessly, and remained open to atypical interventions, such as barricading the street to the school, arranging for parents to pick up their children at a nearby grocery store, and getting volunteers to hand out informative leaflets to folks stopped by the barricade.

Lesson learned? By taking a team approach, I was able to manage the diesel emergency far more skillfully and efficiently than I would have on my own. So the next time you are confronted with a substantial problem, think team.

Figure 1.6 Principal Emergency Checklist

In the event of an emergency, the principal will implement pertinent procedures from the following list:

Fact Gathering:

- ☐ Gather factual details regarding the event (e.g., do not repeat unsubstantiated rumors; do not draw conclusions that other more highly trained professionals should make; do not interview adults/ students if this appears to be a police matter).
- ☐ Obtain information from appropriate sources (e.g., the fire department regarding the extent of fire damage, the parents of a student who is seriously ill or who has died).
- ☐ Determine the extent of the emergency (e.g., Who? What? Where? When? Number and condition of victims?).
- ☐ Obtain parental consent for the release of sensitive information.

Notification:

- ☐ Notify the superintendent of the emergency. If not available, notify the following district administrators in the order listed: superintendent's secretary, assistant superintendent, and business manager.
- ☐ Notify principals and counselors at other district schools and keep them informed.
- ☐ Notify the school emergency team of the situation and schedule a response planning meeting (i.e., specify date, time, location). Identify a regular meeting place and time for future meetings.
- ☐ Arrange for the school district's communications director to handle the media (e.g., TV, radio, the press) and requests for information.
- ☐ Notify school staff members of the emergency by scheduling an information meeting or, if school is out of session, implementing the emergency phone tree. Keep staff informed by sending e-mail news breaks (keep messages short, omit sensitive information). Final note: Direct staff not to post in-house newsbreaks in social networks.
- ☐ Notify students of the emergency situation—using a prepared script—by visiting classrooms, preparing an announcement, or scheduling small group meetings.
- ☐ Notify staff that has family members (e.g., children, spouse) at schools where there is an emergency taking place.

Response Planning Meeting

- ☐ Explain the extent of the emergency and identify the appropriate emergency response.
- ☐ Appoint a recorder for meetings, incoming and outgoing calls, and personal contacts.

☐ Develop a response plan, using the emergency procedures identified in this handbook as a guide, and assign responsibilities.
☐ Determine whether school should be suspended temporarily because of the emergency.
☐ Create scripts for the staff members who will be handling the media, taking incoming phone calls, notifying students, and informing parents.
☐ Arrange for identification badges for non-staff members who will be assisting with the emergency.

Orientation

☐ Faculty:

Hold a faculty meeting to share current information.

Review facts and dispel rumors.

Present plans for reporting information to students and responding to concerns.

Ask teachers if they need assistance talking to students.

Identify faculty and student counseling rooms.

Ask staff members to inform the secretaries if they need a substitute.

Remind staff not to respond to requests for information from the media or parents.

Tell staff to only distribute authorized information.

☐ Student:

Provide information about the crisis, as seems appropriate, given student ages.

Announce the location of the student counseling room.

Tell students to let their teacher know if they need support.

Ask the students to respect the privacy of the persons involved in the crisis.

Direct students not to talk to the media.

☐ Parents:

Prepare a script for persons handling parent phone calls.

Distribute an informational bulletin to parents.

Announce available counseling services.

Response Plan

☐ Follow the emergency specific procedures outlined in the Emergency Handbook.

(Figure continues on next page.)

- ☐ Set up a command post (e.g., by a phone if possible, staffed by an emergency team member); log incoming and outgoing calls. (Note: Do not route calls through to classrooms during the duration of the emergency.)
- ☐ Notify emergency services (e.g., police, fire department) and the superintendent of the location of the command post and who is in charge at that location.
- ☐ Develop a fact sheet for the person handling the media.
- ☐ Call for emergency medical personnel, when needed, and give the location of the injured and/or the command post. If a student or staff member must be transported to a hospital, send another staff person along to act as a liaison between the school, the hospital staff, and family of the victim.
- ☐ Control access to emergency area (e.g., appoint "security" personnel).
- ☐ Designate areas for faculty and student counseling and a staff member who will keep a log of students and staff members requesting services.
- ☐ Remind staff to use the prepared script when responding to student and parent questions; emphasize that staff members are not to talk to media representatives.
- ☐ Assemble appropriate communication tools (e.g., 2-way radios, bullhorn, whistles, and cell phones).
- ☐ Acquire pertinent emergency equipment (e.g., flashlights, first aid kits, blankets).
- ☐ Secure substitute teachers and paraprofessionals as needed.
- ☐ If the emergency occurs when school is not in session, seek permission from the superintendent to utilize the school as a counseling center.
- ☐ Request extra counselors from school district and regional schools. Counselors can assist by monitoring the halls, staying with the victim's class throughout the day, staffing the faculty and student counseling rooms, making pertinent parent contacts, and giving personal assistance to individuals needing support).
- ☐ Instruct secretaries and support staff to keep a record of student releases.

Closure and Debriefing

- ☐ Invite staff to gather at the end of the day to discuss the situation.
- ☐ Give the faculty any additional information and dispel lingering rumors.
- ☐ Identify needs that still need to be addressed.
- ☐ Meet with emergency team members at the end of the day to assess how students and staff are handling the emergency.
- ☐ Critique the emergency team's response to the emergency.

Empower Potential Problem Solvers

When my husband and I remodeled our "new" home—a classic fixer upper—we did most of the work ourselves. After "gutting" the house we upgraded its flooring, ceiling, wall surfaces, plumbing, lighting, and cabinetry. There were a few exceptions, however, such as putting on a custom metal roof and replacing the home's electrical system. These projects were hired out to independent contractors who had the specialized training and experience needed to do the job efficiently and correctly. This approach also saved us mountains of time.

At school I use the independent contractor approach to get help with special projects and all the problems associated with them. My "independent contractors" are staff members with the expertise I need and the willingness to take on extra responsibilities in exchange for the satisfaction that comes from doing stimulating work. I also throw in some modest incentives such as time off, a flex schedule, or, in some cases, a few hours extra pay.

Who are my independent contractors? Several examples follow:

Staff Member	Expertise
Secretary A	Student Attendance Truancy Petitions Truancy Court Hearings
Secretary B	Bus Routes and Schedules Fiscal Management Student Database
Teacher A	Data Analysis Schoolwide Scheduling
Teacher B	Instructional Software Internet Educational Programs
Paraprofessional A	Student Safety Patrol Schedules, Training, and Supervision
Paraprofessional B	Student Behavior Training
Teacher on Special Assignment	Electronic Grade Book & Report Card Math & Writing Testing Oral Reading Fluency Screenings Grades 3–5 State Assessments
PE Specialist	Technology: Computers & Printers Photography Document Cameras

Some of these staff members developed their expertise on their own, but most were encouraged to get specialized training. Regardless, when the aptitude and interest are there, I am delighted to delegate responsibilities to talented staff members. Shared responsibility broadens staff leadership skills, enhances the quality of project implementation, and expands the number of problem-solvers in my school.

What kinds of projects do I assign? Here are a couple of examples:

Secretary A, Attendance Expertise	Prepare truancy petitions, gather supporting evidence, and represent the school in court
Teacher A, Scheduling Expertise	Create the daily, specialist, recess, and lunch schedules in collaboration with other staff members

In regards to problems, here are the types of concerns I routinely delegate to my independent contractors:

Staff Member	Expertise	Problems Handled
Secretary A	Student Attendance Truancy Petitions Truancy Court Hearings	Monitoring students with poor attendance, contacting parents about children with excessive absences, defending truancy petitions in court
Secretary B	Bus Routes and Schedules Fiscal Recordkeeping Student Database	Checking on late busses, finding missing bus students, researching order errors, fixing database glitches
Teacher A	Data Analysis School Scheduling	Finding assessment data errors, solving scheduling snafus
Teacher B	Instructional Software Internet Programs	Correcting software malfunctions, solving Internet access difficulties
Paraprofessional A	Student Safety Patrol Schedules, Training, and Supervision	Solving patrol schedule problems, handling student patrol "no shows," contacting the police regarding vehicular violations
Paraprofessional B	Student Behavior Training	Reviewing school rules with noncompliant students, defusing angry students

Staff Member	Expertise	Problems Handled
Teacher on Special Assignment	Electronic Report Cards Electronic Grade Book	Solving data entry and retrieval problems
Specialist	Technology Photography	Responding to computer hardware and digital camera malfunctions

I respect the work these staff members perform and value the help I get with problems. I have a huge school and cannot hope to handle every difficulty. So when I delegate I don't micromanage—I stay out of the way.

Why would anyone take on extra projects and problems? These individuals are highly dedicated souls who thrive on the stimulation and variety added responsibilities offer. These future school leaders are priceless—empower them.

Suggested Reading

Beatty, Carol A., & Scott, Brenda Barker. (2004). *Building smart teams: A roadmap to high performance.* Thousand Oaks, CA: Sage Publications.

Summing Up

- Access the power of personal interviews to uncover your school's strengths and the areas that need fine-tuning.
- Open your eyes to current or potential facility problems by intentionally "surveying the scene."
- Use staff surveys regularly to assess the quality of school systems, services, and programs.
- Triage the problems you encounter by establishing problem-solving priorities.
- Bring a team approach to complex problems.
- Invite talented staff members to take on stimulating projects and problems.

Making Connections

- Are you overwhelmed with problems? How do you manage the overload in order to stay on top of things? Is your current approach working for you? What should you do differently?
- Do you bring a team approach to school problems? Why or why not? What have been your successes?

Strengthening Professional Practice

- Make a list of the major problems you currently face. Sort them using the following categories: Level I: Health and Safety; Level 2: Student Welfare; and Level 3: School Operation and Mission. Did the categories work for you? How would you modify them to fit your situation?
- Review your list of categorized problems. Within each category, consider *urgency* and *impact*. Which problems would you tackle first given these two considerations? Why?

Theme 2

Counteracting Workplace Negativity

> *Our sense of engagement and satisfaction at work results in large part from the hundreds and hundreds of daily interactions we have while there, whether with a supervisor, colleagues, or customers. The accumulation and frequency of positive versus negative moments largely determines our satisfaction and ability to perform....*
>
> — Daniel Goleman (2006, p. 279)

How can you tell that a workplace has become *negative*? Does the number of *Dilbert* cartoons tacked to the staff bulletin board provide a clue or does one search for furtive-looking staff members speaking *sotto voce* in the hallways? I started my investigation into workplace negativity by consulting my most reliable dictionary. I found these enlightening descriptors for *negative*: hostility, attacking, refusal, criticism, contradictory, disagreeable, pessimism, withdrawal (Merriam-Webster's, 2008, p. 829). I pictured a shouting match between a couple of hostile teachers at one end of the spectrum, and at the other end, educators who have become *so* disengaged they hide behind their computers playing electronic solitaire. Do these pictures of workplace dysfunction seem too extreme? Sadly, I have encountered both scenarios.

According to Lopper, workplace negativity includes "low morale, workplace stress, loss of motivation, and absenteeism" which translates into a working climate characterized by "complaints, criticism, and cynicism" (2008, p. 1). Some school leaders would add the following disheartening attributes to Lopper's list: static student achievement, lackluster teacher performance, unprofessional conduct, contentious staff relationships, and negative talk about one's career, colleagues, and clients. Heathfield observes that "nothing affects employee morale more insidiously than persistent workplace negativity. It saps the energy of your organization and diverts attention away from work and performance" (2009, p. 1). How much negativity should a school leader tolerate? In a word—none.

Fortunately, the tips discussed in this Theme are proven strategies for confronting workplace negativity. You learn how to engage staff in constructive behaviors, nurture a culture of positiveness, curtail negative behavior, and build constructive employee behaviors. The payoff? School relationships that are healthy, supportive, and productive.

Cultivate Constructive Actions

My father was raised on a bustling 150-acre dairy farm where the maxim "busy hands are happy hands" was taken to heart. When my dad left his family's homestead to become a machinist for the airline industry, he started a small but demanding farm operation on the side. I grew up on this mini-farm and by the time I was twelve could cook; sew; bake; put up jam; raise rabbits, chickens, and goats; and grow a cornucopia of fruits and vegetables. I had three active, articulate, assertive siblings but squabbles were few and far between—we had too much work to do.

When I became a school principal I observed that just like on a farm, negativity is diminished when there is productive and engaging work. The direction for this work comes from many sources—federal legislation, state mandates, school district initiatives, and community expectations. There are also enlightening resources to guide school leaders who want to involve staff in improving performance, such as the *Nine Characteristics of High-Performing Schools* (Shannon & Blysma, 2007) and the *School Improvement Planning Process Guide* (OSPI, 2005).

The *Nine Characteristics of High-Performing Schools* provides educators with a sizable "to-do" list of school improvement actions organized by theme (p. v):

Nine Characteristics of High-Performing Schools

- Clear and shared focus
- High standards and expectations
- Effective relationships
- Collaboration and communication
- Alignment with state standards
- Monitoring of learning and teaching
- Focused professional development
- Supportive learning environment
- Family and community involvement

Each theme comes with a descriptive definition, such as the one that follows (p. 27):

> **Clear and Shared Focus**
>
> Everybody knows where they are going and why.
>
> The focus is on achieving a shared vision, and all understand their role in achieving the vision. The focus and vision are developed from common beliefs and values, creating a consistent direction for all involved.

In addition to the aforementioned list of actions and definitions, there are suggested surveys for staff, students, parents, and community members. The results generated by these surveys will help principals assess their school's progress toward meeting each of the nine characteristics.

The *School Improvement Planning Process Guide* serves as a companion to the nine characteristics sourcebook. In addition to process steps and surveys, it offers data tools and professional practice recommendations.

The *Nine Characteristics of High-Performing Schools* and the *School Improvement Planning Process Guide* provide endless opportunities for productive and rewarding work. As an added bonus, keeping staff members *constructively* engaged is a powerful antidote to workplace negativity.

Suggested Readings

Office of the Superintendent of Public Instruction. (2005). *School improvement planning: Process guide*. Olympia, WA: Author. Available at http://www.k12.wa.us/Improvement/publications/SIPGuide/SIPGuide.pdf.

Shannon, G. Sue, & Bylsma, Pete. (2007). *The nine characteristics of high-performing schools*, 2nd ed. Olympia, WA: Office of the Superintendent of Public Instruction. Available at http://www.k12.wa.us/research/pubdocs/NineCharacteristics.pdf.

Affirm

My high school choir teacher was passionate about classical music and played snippets of noteworthy symphonies at the start of every class. Students were challenged to identify the symphony or composer—rarely could anyone name both—and success merited an abundance of praise. One day *Scheherazade* was featured—a symphonic suite composed by Rimsky-Korsakov. As luck would have it, this was the *only* classical recording my folks owned and it was regularly played in our home. When *Scheherazade* began, my hand shot up immediately and when called upon, I confidently named the music *and* the composer. My astounded choir teacher and classmates enthusiastically applauded my success and from that day forward, I took a keen interest in classical music. I think about my choir teacher when I need to strengthen employee conduct in my school. Not surprisingly, positive affirmations are a powerful tool for eliciting positive behavior.

What kind of behavior are we after? Schools and school districts spell out behavior expectations through professional standards, job descriptions, new employee checklists, evaluation criteria, staff norms, and even logos like "Students First" or "We Climb Higher." But once these guidelines have been presented to staff members, then what? Wise school leaders look for ways to *affirm* behaviors that positively impact their schools. Here are five easy ways to do just that:

- *Person to Person Communication:* Take time to personally thank staff members for behaviors that give a boost to school culture and climate. All it takes are a few well-chosen words and a sincere attitude.
- *Written Messages:* Use e-mail messages or handwritten "good news notes" to praise teachers' relationship-enhancing behaviors. A couple of lines like "Great job making your new student feel welcomed," are all you need to make a lasting impression.
- *Public Announcements:* Use faculty bulletins, newsletter articles, school board reports, electronic news breaks, and staff meeting announcements to *publicly* applaud staff members for positive contributions. Highlight employees who mentor new staff members, serve on student intervention teams, or "go the extra mile" during emergencies.
- *Time-Off Tickets:* Thank staff members for exemplary behavior by distributing tickets that allow staff members to leave school early—be willing to cover a class if necessary. This gift of time gives a morale boost, builds lasting relationships, and generates untold good will.
- *Observation and Evaluation Reports:* Document positive behaviors and attitudes in employee observation and evaluation write ups. Be sure to be specific about the behaviors you appreciate.

Figure 2.1 is a simple format for affirming desired behaviors in a teacher final evaluation. Note that the teacher is reinforced for engaging in professional growth activities, providing school and community service, and accomplishing goals. The teacher's culture building behaviors are also identified, such as leading book studies, mentoring colleagues, and developing a student and parent friendly classroom.

Figure 2.1. Final Evaluation Summary

Final Evaluation for ____________________

Prepared by: ____________________

- Principal–Teacher Professional Development Activities
  - Progress Conferences: September 10, January 22, June 8
  - Preplanned Observations: October 13 & March 15
  - Informal Observations: *See Principal's Visitation Log*
- Teacher's Professional Growth Activities
  - In-service: Reading coursework, math in-service, state assessment training, hands-on science workshop
  - Visitations: Observed 2 teachers (Focus: student writing)
  - Professional Reading: *The 4 Core Factors for School Success* by Todd Whitaker and Jeffrey Zoul (Larchmont, NY: Eye On Education, 2008)
- School & Community Service
  - Grade-level team meeting coordinator
  - Principal advisory committee member
  - Associated student body advisor
  - City Council member
- Teacher's Goal Accomplishments
  - Raising student achievement in reading and math
  - Improving student attitudes toward school and learning
  - Nurturing grade-level collaboration
  - Leading a teacher book study: *The 4 Core Factors for School Success*
  - Mentoring a new teacher and a university practicum student
- Strengths Identified by Principal
  - Teaching (e.g., intentional implementation of required curriculum, clarity and enthusiasm of presentation, variation of lesson design, engagement of students, and assessment of student learning)

(Figure continues on next page.)

- Growing professionally through coursework, special projects, and mentoring colleagues
- Creating a student and parent oriented learning environment (e.g., attractive, friendly, welcoming)
- Developing excellent rapport with students and eliciting positive attitudes and responsible behaviors
- Promoting the growth of children with challenging learning deficits and/or behaviors

♦ Principal Goals:

Continue to support schoolwide goals by:

- Teaching the adopted reading and math programs with fidelity
- Implementing the new state standards in math and science
- Continuing to serve as a positive and constructive role model

♦ Final Comment:

It has been a pleasure working with __________ this year. She is an excellent teacher who goes above and beyond to contribute to school and district goals. As importantly, she models positive and constructive behaviors that go a long way toward making our school a positive environment for both students and staff.

Date: ____________ Teacher: ________________________________

Date: ____________ Principal: ________________________________

When was the last time *your* positive contributions were affirmed? Recall how you felt and the motivation you received to continue down this positive pathway. Give your staff this same experience by affirming behavior that helps *your* school move away from negativity towards positiveness.

Showcase Relationship Role Models

In her landmark book *10 Traits of Highly Effective Schools*, McEwan describes positive relationships as "the glue that holds the school together" and "the lubricant that makes everything in the school run smoothly" (2009, p. 77). Positive relationships are also affirmed in Harwayne's inspiring book *Going Public*, which describes the development of the innovative literacy program at the Manhattan New School. Harwayne highlighted the "spirit of generosity" among the school's teachers and the uplifting "social tone": "Those of us who are fortunate enough to call the Manhattan New School home know what accounts for that very special feeling. We come to work filled with joy and compassion, as well as devotion to the work we do and the people we work alongside of" (1999, pp. 102–103).

Every school leader wants laudatory staff relationships but how do you get them? One way is to showcase staff members who *are* relationship pros. I feature these gems in newsletter articles titled *My First Job* and the *Teacher Q & A*.

My First Job puts the spotlight on exemplary classified staff members. Selected employees respond to interview questions about their current position and their very first job (Figure 2.2, page 39).

Excerpts from an interview with Seana Moran, a dedicated Washington Reading Corp volunteer, highlights her positive regard for and relationships with students:

> **Current Position:** I manage volunteer and student data, assist in tracking student progress, provide reading interventions and materials for my team members' tutoring sessions, and plan Family Literacy Nights. I enjoy all my responsibilities.
>
> **Favorite Part:** Working with the students—I tutor a delightful group of first graders. It is wonderful to see their faces when they finally understand how to sound out words!
>
> **First Job:** I was a dietary aide at a rehabilitation center.

What I Learned: I quickly learned that "dietary aide" was just a fancy title for dishwasher and what I really wanted to do was work with people. I love helping others and this compassion spread to children. I am now working to become a Special Education teacher. My first job may not have been glamorous but I learned what I really enjoy doing and about the person I wished to become.

Praiseworthy role models are also featured in teacher interviews (Figure 2.3, page 40). In the excerpts that follow Figure 2.3 (page 40), note how the teachers radiate enthusiasm and relationship building attitudes.

Figure 2.2. My First Job

Current Position:

____

____

____

____

Favorite Part:

____

____

____

____

First Job:

____

____

____

____

How I Got the Job:

____

____

____

____

What I Learned:

____

____

____

____

Figure 2.3. Teacher Q & A

What do you like most about your job?

____

____

What's your biggest challenge?

____

____

What are you most proud of?

____

____

Who are your heroes?

____

____

If you weren't a teacher what would you be doing?

____

____

How do you relax?

____

____

What's your favorite meal? Whom would you invite to share it?

____

____

What are you reading?

____

____

Naomi Conner, 5th Grade Teacher

- What do you like most about your job?

  I enjoy having a job that is so inspiring and rewarding. I love watching my students grow both academically and emotionally over the school year. It is a blessing to be in a career that allows me to make a difference!

- Who are your heroes?

  My parents—they are always there to support me. I appreciated them growing up, but now that I have my own children I have a greater understanding of their unconditional love and devotion. I have especially appreciated watching them as grandparents to my children and my brother's children.

Joelle Wright, 2nd Grade Teacher

- What do you like about your job?

  I get to still be a kid. It's *cool* to read children's books. I get to be creative with art projects and its fun modeling for children how to use your imagination and see the world from a different perspective.

- Whom do you admire most?

  Selfless people who love to serve others; people who are able to laugh at themselves and find pleasure in the small things; and people that use a turn signal when driving!

Valerie Anderson, 5th Grade Teacher

- Do you have a major goal this school year?

  Yes—to align my math teaching with the new state standards. I am also going to implement a goal setting and monitoring program to help my students in reading, math, and writing.

- Whom do you admire?

  Harold Sigler, my middle school English teacher. He taught me that teaching was more than the classroom content, that it was caring about *each* individual student.

When you showcase relationship experts you announce to others what you value. The people you feature feel honored and provide sterling role models for others to emulate.

Be Efficient

I knew a principal who tried to boost morale by purchasing donuts for his faculty on a weekly basis. His staff, although appreciative of his generous gesture, remained dispirited. Why? The principal had failed to detect the underlying cause of low morale in his school—inefficiency. The principal's staff endured endless scheduling snafus, missed deadlines, and time-wasting meetings. They would have gladly traded in the pastries for a modicum of efficiency.

One way to keep a school running smoothly is through the use of electronic bulletins and news breaks. I prepare mine using publishing software so that I can incorporate colorful headings and eye-catching graphics. The bulletin for the upcoming week is e-mailed on Friday and includes these features:

- *This Week:* Lists activities for the coming week, such as meetings, assemblies, spirit days, and concerts.
- *Upcoming Events:* Announces events scheduled for the next two months.
- *Due:* Gives deadlines for reports, testing, social dues, and other staff obligations.
- *Emergency Drills:* Reminds teachers to prepare their students for fire, earthquake, lockdown, and hazardous spill drills.
- *Birthdays:* The current month's classified and certificated birthdays are announced (e.g., Cathie, May 7th).
- *It's Your Turn:* Lists staff members assigned to KP duty and teachers responsible for filling the front hall display case with student work.
- *News You Can Use:* Tells staff about flyers that have arrived regarding degree programs, student contests, and field trip opportunities. The flyers are filed in a staff room crate titled *News You Can Use.*
- *Websites Worth Watching:* Gives URLs for curriculum, in-service, or free resources.
- *Quips & Quotes:* Provides inspiring quotes or amusing remarks from famous authors, educators, and celebrities.
- *Special Features:* Includes teacher interviews about instructional practice, excerpts from current education books, and research highlights.

Electronic "news breaks" cover information that can't wait for the Friday bulletin, such as announcing a grant opportunity, a contest winner, or a meeting cancellation. Staff bulletins and news breaks keep staff members up to date and organized—a definite morale booster (West, 1997).

Thoughtfully engineered faculty meetings also give staff attitudes a lift. In *Power-up Staff Meetings,* the fifth tip in Theme 5, you will learn how to efficiently handle school improvement projects through a series of short, well- designed faculty meetings. Check out Figures 5.10 through 5.12 (pages 129–131), which provide examples of successful meeting agendas. Sometimes, however, it is preferable to get staff members working independently, so in lieu of the traditional principal-directed meeting, I schedule a "center meeting." Teachers find ten to fifteen stations set up in our library and at each there is a task to complete, such as filling out a questionnaire, responding to a poll, signing up for committee work, or jotting down ideas for the next school improvement plan (West, 1995). Teachers visit the centers in any order and depart as soon as their work is finished. Center meetings are an efficient—and popular—way for staff members to complete a variety of school improvement and housekeeping tasks (Figures 2.4 on page 44, 2.5 on page 45, and 2.6 on page 46).

Well-crafted communiqués and thoughtfully engineered meetings will help your school operate efficiently and give a vital boost to staff morale. Although donuts are always nice touch, make efficiency your top priority.

(Text continues on page 47.)

Figure 2.4. August Center Meeting Tasks

Center #1	Staff Room Schedule Sign up for cleanup duty and the opportunity to bring treats.
Center #2	Science Instruction Input What do you need to be successful?
Center #3	Principal Advisory Committee Grade level reps are still needed. Can you serve?
Center #4	Coffee Drinkers Jot down your name for a turn to bring a can of coffee.
Center #5	Display Case Assignments Months have been assigned. Please pick your theme.
Center #6	Field Trips Specify destination and educational outcomes.
Center #7	Book Study Opportunities Five fabulous books are suggested; rank order by interest.
Center #8	Teacher Evaluations Check out the new evaluation criteria. Any suggestions?
Center #9	Teacher Goal Plans Complete your goal plan for the year.
Center #10	Principal's Mission What's your take on the principal's mission?

Figure 2.5. Center 5: Science Instruction Input

At this station you will find a copy of the new state science curriculum. Note the targets for your grade level. What do you need to be a successful science teacher? Jot your ideas below:

Grade Level	Preparation	Resources
	What do you need to prepare? Who do you want to consult with? What training do you need?	What kinds of teaching materi-als and tools do you need ?
K		
Gr. 1		
Gr. 2		
Gr. 3		
Gr. 4		
Gr. 5		
Gr. 6		

Figure 2.6. Center 13: Principal's Mission

Based upon your contact with and observations of the principal (at staff meetings, interviews, goal conferences, school improvement & curriculum meetings; via weekly bulletins, observation feedback reports, etc.), what do you think is the principal's mission at our school?

Jot your answer below and place your response in the provided envelope.

Thank you!

Orchestrate

Gerald Murphy, a talented American painter, and his wife Sara explored the *avant-garde* art world in Europe between the two world wars. After acquiring a villa in France, Gerald and Sara invited into their home an extraordinary collection of *new wave* artists, musicians, dancers, and writers. Among these illuminati were F. Scott Fitzgerald, Ernest Hemingway, Cole Porter, Pablo Picasso, Fernand Léger, Dorothy Parker, and Igor Stravinsky (Vaill, 1998).

Gerald was the consummate entertainer and when he invited noteworthy figures into his home, he left nothing to chance. He could be seen "circulating among his guests, introducing this one to that, starting a conversation here, changing a subject there—a friend later describes him as 'stage manag[ing] his parties down to the last detail, right down to what stories people should tell'" (Vaill,1998, p. 4).

There is a lesson to be learned from Gerald Murphy's esoteric social orchestration. Sometimes you need to get the *right* people, talking about the *right* things, to the *right* people. You can defuse negativity in a school, for example, by orchestrating *what* will be said to *whom*. Teacher–principal goal conferences provide the perfect opportunity. I schedule goal conferences that bring together four to six teachers with diverse talents, personalities, and outlooks. When I am selecting teachers for these groups I mix those who become easily discouraged with the go-getters, negative talkers with the optimists, and naysayers with the cheerleaders. The enthusiasm and accomplishments of the *positive* teachers gives a lift to those less inspired.

Prior to the conference the teachers submit a Teacher Goal Plan (Figure 2.7, page 48). I read the teachers' plans with a highlighter in hand so that I can flag the goals that I want teachers to share. This is a crucial step when you are striving to bring out the best in each staff member. If at the goal conference you throw out a nonspecific question like "What are your goals this year?," the negatively inclined teachers may respond with "Just to survive!" If, on the other hand, you ask teachers to talk about a *specific* goal, such as improving student's writing style, the teachers will skip the flip remark in favor of talking about writing.

I use the same concept with my positive teachers only in regards to ideas I want them to *advance*. I asked a whiz with classroom assessments, for example, to show how he crafts interim tests from internet sources and uses the results to monitor students' math skills. His innovative assessment practice quickly caught on with other teachers.

Engineering staff interactions takes advanced planning but is worth the effort. When teachers' novel ideas and effervescent outlooks impress their colleagues, it's gold.

Figure 2.7. Teacher Goal Planning Form

Professional Growth Activities

Check (√) the activities that you plan to engage in during the school year. Add specifics (e.g., name of workshop, courses, or books) if you have them:

- ☐ Observe Other Teachers: ____________________
- ☐ Attend Workshops: ____________________
- ☐ Complete Graduate Level Coursework: ____________________
- ☐ Read Professional Books/Journals: ____________________

School & District Service

Will you boost your professional growth by serving on a committee this year? Please specify"

- ☐ School Committees: ____________________
- ☐ District Committees: ____________________

Goals and Special Projects

List your major goals and projects: ____________________

____

____

____

____

____

____

____

____

____

Teacher/Specialist: ____

Conference Dates: ____ Fall ____ Winter ____ Spring

Put Out Fires

Blunders, snafus, and glitches are a part of organizational life. If you fix them in a timely fashion you score points with staff members and keep your organization on an even keel; if you *don't* you invite disorder and negativity flare-ups. The example that follows is a case in point.

A few days before a series of science events—involving students, teachers, and parents at my school and a nearby elementary—my teachers and I received the event schedule from the organizers, a well-meaning but harried teacher committee. The schedule had been created at the last minute and it showed. The committee had neglected to align the event schedule with recess and lunch periods, teacher prep times, and evening events. Consequently, there were sizable problems: students scheduled for assemblies during recesses; speakers assigned to cafeterias during lunch periods; teachers asked to supervise students on their prep breaks; and evening programs located in gyms already booked for community basketball. Worse than the schedule, however, were the strident e-mails that teachers began firing at committee members; messages like: "What on earth were you thinking!" In self-defense the committee members fired back with their *own* complaints, such as: "Where were *you* when we needed help!"

The frustrated teachers, including the committee members, had violated a prime organizational rule that is, in actuality, a Japanese proverb: "Fix the problem not the blame" (Anonymous, 2009).

I contacted the principal of the other school and "fixing the problem" became our mission. We sent a joint e-mail calling a halt to the complaints, directing teachers to be professional, and assuring everyone that the schedule would be revised. Then we assigned a teacher who is a scheduling genius to help the committee fix the scheduling snafu. By the following morning, a corrected schedule was distributed along with updated program announcements. The fire was quickly put out and the staff soon regained their positive focus.

There is another kind of flare-up that needs to be addressed quickly: the negativity emanating from individual staff members. The negativity may include hurtful gossip, cutting remarks about colleagues or school administrators, or derisive comments about students or their parents. Seldom does the disgruntled staff member express negative views directly to or in front of the principal. Principals usually hear about the problem from other staff members who want something done about it but, understandably, do *not* want to be named as sources.

My first response is to spend more time around the negative staff member so that I will hear unprofessional remarks first hand. If I do, I schedule a meeting to review expectations. But what if I *never* hear an unprofessional remark? Then I look for other signs of negativity such as inadequate teaching, failure to meet professional goals, lackluster participation in staff and curriculum meetings, or high absenteeism. Problems like these open the door for supportive and corrective conversations about professionalism.

Addressing organizational snafus and unprofessional behavior quickly and competently keeps your school positive. So the next time you have a negativity flare-up, be a good fire fighter.

Suggested Readings

Barth, Roland S. (2003). *Lessons learned: Shaping relationships and the culture of the workplace*. Thousand Oaks, CA: Corwin Press.

Edmonson, Stacey, Combs, Julie, & Harris, Sandra. (2008). *Managing conflict: 50 Strategies for school leaders*. Larchmont, NY: Eye On Education.

Summing Up

- Counteract negativity by engaging staff members in constructive work.
- Affirm positive, contributing behaviors.
- Put the spotlight on relationship role models.
- Enhance efficiency to boost staff morale.
- Orchestrate positive conversations.
- Respond quickly and competently when negativity arises.

Making Connections

- How do you keep staff members focused on important work? Do you revisit goals and objectives? Is time scheduled to accomplish stated goals? What changes do you need to make?
- Do you respond quickly to signs of negativity? What actions do you take? Are they effective? Why or why not?

Strengthening Professional Practice

- Try out the center meeting concept: make a list of tasks, create the center instructions and documents, and schedule a meeting time. After the meeting, evaluate the outcome. For example, was this an efficient way to get multiple tasks completed? Did staff members remain engaged? Would you try this format again?

- How are other principals in your school district handling staff negativity? Schedule a meeting to share ideas.

Theme 3

Stopping Staff Misconduct

Actions not words, define our rules.
— MacKenzie (2003, p. 79)

As a rule, the people who work in schools are thoughtful, ethical, and responsible individuals. Nevertheless, they are also human and may make a minor mistake or two from fatigue, overwork, forgetfulness, or confusion about expectations. The false steps of these employees are easily handled—a quick correction is all it takes to get them back on track. But what if the mistakes become chronic or grow in significance? What if a staff member knowingly fails to perform a required duty, for example, or observe school policy? What if the employee goes even further and refuses to carry out a directive or does something illegal? These kinds of behaviors fall into the category of *staff misconduct* and they require immediate action.

Staff misconduct covers a potpourri of personnel problems: "unexcused absences and excessive tardiness; neglect of duty; abusive, insulting, or profane language; corporal punishment; insubordination; sexual misconduct; illegal use of a controlled substance; thefts and fraud; and criminal misconduct" (Lawrence & Vachon, 2003, p. 5). Sound alarming? Take a deep breath and hold on—there are steps you can take to *prevent* employee misconduct or stop it in its tracks.

The strategies covered in this Theme address staff misconduct proactively. You learn how to keep staff members properly informed of their responsibilities, create conduct norms, elicit responsible behaviors, and intervene when you fail to get compliance. There are also guidelines to follow should you believe disciplinary action to be just around the corner.

Although this Theme puts the spotlight on staff misconduct, it intentionally does *not* address performance concerns that are handled through the supervision and evaluation process. In regards to a teacher, for example, these concerns might include poor instructional technique, inadequate assessment methods, improper implementation of adopted instructional programs, and ineffective student management. Contact your human resources director for help with these kinds of problems.

The information presented in this Theme should *not* be construed as legal advice. This section of the book provides tips for preventing staff misconduct; it is neither a primer on school law nor a discourse on employee discipline procedures. When you encounter staff misconduct, notify your human resources director and your superintendent immediately. These administrators will oversee the actions you take and get you the legal advice you need.

Meanwhile, bring an optimistic approach to supervising your staff members. There is a lot you can do to nurture professionalism and keep staff misconduct from becoming an unwelcome presence in your school.

Spell It Out

When I was a teen I landed a job grading apples and arrived for my first day of work with a knot in my stomach. Other than slicing up pippins for pie, I didn't know the first thing about apples. Fortunately, my boss was an employee training pro. My orientation included touring the apple orchard and the packing shed; learning apple-grading terminology and criteria; comparing appropriately sized, unblemished apples to culls—fruit rejects; and observing experienced graders in action. Thanks to my thoughtful boss, when I was finally assigned to one of the grading tables I was well prepared and confident.

As a principal responsible for supervising a vast array of staff members, I keep in mind how I learned the ropes as an apple grader. I similarly nurture the success of new employees by spelling out their duties in detail. This endeavor begins with an in-depth orientation meeting where a variety of issues are addressed, from job responsibilities to district policies and procedures (Figure 3.1, page 56). Plenty of time is scheduled for this initial orientation and veteran teachers are recruited to help orient the newbie's. Teacher leaders enjoy providing school tours, serving as mentors, and explaining how to use adopted curriculum. Pairing new teachers with veterans also starts the faculty bonding process.

It is helpful to provide new staff members with references they can refer back to. The tools I use include the following:

- District Strategic Plan
- School Improvement Plan
- School Performance Report
- Curriculum Standards
- Student Assessment Guide
- Instructional Materials List
- Supervision & Evaluation Guide
- Student-Parent Handbook
- Staff Roster
- Facility Map
- State Professional Standards for Educators
- Staff Conduct Norms (Figure 3.3, page 64)
- Position Description
- Certificated Check-in Packet (Figure 3.2, page 57)
- School Schedules
- Staff Handbook
- Field Trip Guidelines (Figure 3.4, page 67)
- Student Discipline Guide
- Emergency Handbook (Theme 4)

One of the most valuable tools is the *Certificated Check-in Packet* (Figure 3.2, page 57) which not only gives teachers a guide to opening school but also reminds teachers of student care and safety obligations. Note that the packet is signed and returned to document that teachers have been informed of their responsibilities.

Figure 3.1. New Teacher Topics

Professional Expectations

- ☐ State Professional Standards for Educators
- ☐ Principal Expectations for Teachers
- ☐ Staff Code of Conduct

Supervision & Evaluation

- ☐ Progress Conferences: Fall, Winter, Spring
- ☐ Formal Observations, Instructional Frameworks
- ☐ Drop-in Classroom Visits
- ☐ Professional Growth Opportunities

Curriculum & Instruction

- ☐ State Curriculum Standards
- ☐ State Assessments
- ☐ Instructional Materials

Orders & Budget

- ☐ Supplies
- ☐ Instructional Materials
- ☐ Access to funds

Student Guidance & Discipline

- ☐ Student Expectations
- ☐ Discipline Handbook
- ☐ Progressive Discipline Steps
- ☐ Schoolwide Interventions
- ☐ Office Referrals
- ☐ Schoolwide Intervention Team

Policies and Procedures

- ☐ School Board/District Policies
- ☐ State Education Codes
- ☐ Certificated Check-in Packet
- ☐ Staff Handbook
- ☐ Student & Parent Handbook
- ☐ Emergency Handbook
- ☐ Personal Medical Form
- ☐ School Security

Schedules

- ☐ Daily/Specialist
- ☐ Curriculum

Figure 3.2. Certificated Staff Check-in Packet

Teacher Check-in Packet

Teacher/Specialist: ________________ Assignment: ________________

Mark each item below using the following code: √ = Completed/Reviewed N/A = Not Applicable

Prior to First School Day

___ Notify the office staff regarding ordering problems.

___ Move supply boxes and other freight to your classroom ASAP (send invoices to office).

___ Review August Meeting Schedule—please arrive on time.

___ Only one custodian is on duty so please haul your trash, cardboard, and recycling material to the appropriate dumpsters. Throw out worn instructional materials you no longer want and haul good-quality items to be shared or sold to the storage room.

First Day

___ Wear your **Staff ID Badge**. Remind parents to pick up **Visitor's Badges**.

___ **Specialists:** From 8:00 AM until the first bell, help children find their rooms.

___ **Classroom Teachers:** Between 8:00 and 8:35, be available in your classrooms to greet parents who want to help their children find their classrooms—then direct students and parents to outside line up locations.

On the 2nd day of school, we will follow normal procedures (i.e., children line up outside until the bell rings; parents may walk children to class after the first bell).

___ **Prior to 9:00 AM:** Take attendance using the electronic attendance system. Students must be *physically in attendance* to be counted as present. Notify the office, however, about children who are absent because of illness, vacations, etc.

(Figure continues on next page.)

___ If students appear in your room that are not on your class list, notify the office staff by phone and then send the students to the office.

___ **Prior to 9:00 AM:** Take lunch count and turn in with your attendance. Return the following to the office each morning: **Free & Reduced Price Meal applications, notes about transportation changes, and medical information.**

___ Identify—early in the day—how each child will be traveling home. **Notify** the office about any uncertainties ASAP.

___ **Grade K-1 Teachers:** To speed up the lunch lines, help the cashier out by having your children wear tags **labeled** with their name & student code. Save the tags—you will need them again on days when the cashier is absent and replaced by a substitute.

___ **All Teachers:** Help students learn their **lunch code**. Please also explain that it is a violation to share their codes with other students.

___ Provide your students with **passes** (e.g., office, restroom, health room). Note: Bathroom passes that can be worn around the neck are more hygienic.

___ The school day officially ends at 3:05 but each teacher walks their class to the buses and late bus lines **at 3:00 PM**. Make certain students get on the right buses by escorting them. Because of safety hazards in the bus area, do not release students to walk on their own.

___ Students who are walking or who are being picked up need **green passes** provided by the office. These passes are checked by a specialist before the students can walk to the front of the school. Review this procedure with students.

___ Teach your students how to *walk* in the hallways (e.g., walk in single or double lines, keep voices off, avoid brushing against or touching bulletin boards or displays).

First Week

___ Give a **copy** of your **Discipline Plan** to the principal (include classroom expectations, progressive discipline steps, consequences, and incentives). Parent notification should be part of your list of consequences.

___ On Friday, provide the secretary with the names of students who did not report for school.

___ Our school district has adopted a nutrition policy out of concern for the growing numbers of children who are overweight and/or poorly nourished from eating unhealthy foods. **Teachers may no longer use candy, soda, and other high-sugar foods as rewards.** Teachers may provide healthy snacks, however, such as cheese sticks, low fat/salt popcorn, fruit juice, nuts, trail mix, pretzels, low fat/salt granola bars, and dried fruit. Final Note: **Please don't allow children to eat snacks throughout the day.** This practice often leads to unhealthy weight gains and interferes with healthy eating at lunch time. If you allow snacks, set a short time period for it.

___ Inform Parents: Send parents a letter that introduces yourself and outlines your educational beliefs, goals, and expectations for students and parents (i.e., how parents can support and be involved).

___ **Review & Reinforce with Students:** Tell students about expected character traits (e.g., be responsible, trustworthy, respectful, fair, caring, and a good citizen), behavior expectations (e.g., school, class, playground, bus, assembly), and classroom procedures. The school rules and behavior expectations are outlined in the Student Discipline Handbook.

___ Orient Students: Explain the school recognition programs (e.g., K-3 Talented Tiger, Gr. 4–5 Meet the Principal Lunches, All Here Attendance Coupons, and Tiger Paw Tickets—which are cashed in for entertaining and educational "character building" movies in the spring).

___ Read the updated **Emergency, Staff, Student Discipline,** and **Student–Parent Handbooks**.

___ Practice fire, earthquake, chemical spill, and lock down drills during the month of September. Our expectations are that children will be orderly and silent during drills. Fill out the box below to document your practice drills—this is a new state requirement.

DRILL	DATE	TIME	DURATION
Fire			
Earthquake			
Lock Down			
Chemical Spill			

(Figure continues on next page.)

Second to Fourth Weeks

___ You will be invited to a Professional Goal Conference meeting. Please complete and return the attached Teacher Goal Plan.

___ Complete the **Sub Handbook**. It is easy to use—just fill in the blanks! You may also attach documents to it. One **copy** should be submitted to the head secretary; the **original remains in your room** for the substitute teacher's use. Please keep this handbook up to date.

For Your Protection—and Students' Protection—Read & Follow the Following Liability Provisions:

___ Complete all the tasks outlined in the Certificated Check-in Packet.

___ Maintain a safe and orderly classroom at all times.

___ Report suspected child abuse/neglect to the principal or counselor immediately (i.e., call the office). Ensure that Child Protective Services (CPS) is notified—you may make the call yourself or ask for assistance. Don't forget to complete the required CPS Referral documentation form.

___ Send all medications (prescription & over-the-counter) to the office. Do not dispense medication. Also, do not allow children to self-medicate without authorization from the school district nurse.

___ Check with the school health attendant to see if any of your students require special care because of health conditions.

___ Apply basic first aid to injured or ill students—but keep from using procedures only a medic should employ (e.g., only a trained professional should move children who might have broken bones or suspected back/neck injuries).

___ Supervise students at all times (e.g., do not leave children unattended in hallways or classrooms).

___ Prevent student access to hazardous substances. Store any product that is toxic in cupboards that are locked or completely out of reach of children. Keep only school-labeled products in your classroom **(Health Department regulations do not permit staff to keep store bought cleaners, aerosols, hand wipes, air fresheners, etc. in classrooms or offices). Note: Exceptions may be made for some items if you acquire a Material Safety Data Sheet from the manufacturer. This document must be kept in the school's Material Safety Data Notebook (see secretaries for assistance).**

___ Provide instruction to students regarding dangerous items (e.g., scissors).

___ Keep dangerous teacher equipment (e.g., paper cutters) out of reach of students.

___ Prevent students from moving TVs and other large AV equipment on carts.

___ Never use physical force, corporal punishment, demeaning comments, or a harsh tone of voice to discipline students. Do not withhold food or deny access to the bathroom as disciplinary measures.

___ Report on time for scheduled events and responsibilities.

___ Never send students out early for recess—supervisors may be on breaks.

___ Supervise properly when taking your class out for an extra recess (e.g., keep kids away from the bus area and dumpsters, instruct students about hazards).

___ Do not send students to the recycling bin on the playground at nonrecess times, as no adults will be available to supervise.

___ Ensure that you have an adequate number of chaperones on walking and bus field trips (see Staff Handbook for guidelines). Both walking and bus field trips require completion of the **Field Trip Check List** (see Staff Handbook Appendix).

Review the Following Management Check List:

___ Arrive on time for your work assignment and observe your work hours. The starting time for certificated staff is 8:05 AM and the ending time is 3:35 PM.

(Figure continues on next page.)

___ Read the weekly electronic Staff Bulletin and the periodic News Breaks.

___ Follow the policies and procedures outlined in the following handbooks: Staff, Emergency, Discipline, and Student–Parent.

___ Be on time for meetings—grade level, staff, student services team, schoolwide intervention team.

___ Draft lesson plans 3 days in advance in case of an emergency.

___ **Provide subs with *written* plans**—it is not permissible to phone them in. Complete the substitute evaluation form and return to the principal's mailbox.

___ Give the principal and secretary copies of parent bulletins so that we can include your news (e.g., upcoming events) in staff and parent bulletins.

___ Schedule your special events, in advance, with the principal. Keep the office staff up to date regarding special activities so that they can respond to phone calls from parents.

___ Contact the parents of students with poor attendance and document your calls/conferences by e-mailing a summary of your conversation with the parent to the attendance secretary. This documentation is vital if we have to submit a truancy petition. The dean of students will follow up with additional interventions if poor attendance continues.

___ Cooperate with staff coordinating student health screenings (e.g., head lice, vision, hearing) and testing (e.g., special education, Title I).

Please sign, date, and return this form:

Date: ___________ Signature: ____________________________________

Due to the principal on ______________. Thank you!

Providing a thorough orientation gets teachers up to speed quickly. It also provides a proactive way to deter staff mistakes and misconduct. So take time to spell out your expectations.

Create Conduct Norms

When it comes to troublesome behavior, we can learn a lot from school counselors. These priceless professionals are problem behavior experts. They maintain an optimistic outlook, never give up, and draw from a toolkit full of powerful strategies. One of their most effective techniques is teaching "replacement" behaviors—they show people *what* to do instead of what *not* to do. Adept school leaders use this concept to prevent staff misconduct—they tell their staff members *what* to do by creating conduct norms (West & Derrington, 2009).

Conduct norms are a set of expectations that guide behavior. In the school setting, they cover these types of concerns: interpersonal relationships, climate, professional growth, communications, conflict management, decision making, and operations. To be effective, norms should be crystal clear, like the communication rules that follow:

- Contribute to the effectiveness of staff meetings by arriving on time, listening attentively, avoiding side conversations, and sharing information in a *time-conscious* manner.
- Keep the staff room a pleasant place by wiping up spills, bussing dishes, and sharing clean up duties.
- Observe schedules (e.g., arrive on time for events, vacate shared spaces punctually, and give notice of schedule changes).

When you are ready to draft norms for your school, involve your staff. Developing expectations collaboratively heightens their effectiveness. Staff members know what problem behavior look like and will contribute plenty of ideas. Your employees will also appreciate getting a say in how business is conducted.

Staff involvement need not take an inordinate amount of time. You can develop norms quickly by providing a sample for consideration, such as the guidelines presented in Figure 3.3 (page 64). Distribute these norms at a faculty meeting after arranging staff members into groups of three to four. Working collaboratively, each team assesses the value of each norm using the following code: + = Valuable—keep exactly as worded; √ = Needs fine-tuning (include revision); 0 = Drop it, not necessary.

Bring closure to this activity is by asking a spokesperson from each group to share three expectations: one they *retained* as written, one they

Figure 3.3 Staff Code of Conduct

We will build a quality school, support every student's learning, and nurture professional relationships by following these expectations:

INTERPERSONAL RELATIONS

Recognize that each person brings education, experiences, and talents that are unique and valuable.

Demonstrate that *every* job is important and *every* person is deserving of respect.

Show loyalty by representing staff members and our school positively.

CLIMATE

Create opportunities for team building through schoolwide projects and special activities.

Contribute to school effectiveness by creating an inviting environment, doing our part when help is needed, and maintaining a positive outlook.

Look for humor and laugh a lot.

PROFESSIONAL GROWTH

Stay current with research, implement *best practices*, and grow professionally.

Support the professional growth of colleagues through mentoring, peer coaching, and collaborative planning.

COMMUNICATIONS

Be professional in verbal and written communications.

Share views and collaborate constructively.

Respect confidentiality as it pertains to students, parents, and staff.

Demonstrate that parents are vital partners by keeping them informed about their children's education and progress.

CONFLICT MANAGEMENT

Employ conflict resolution strategies (e.g., "I" messages, agreeing to disagree, facilitators) when concerns arise.

Use *face to face* communication—not e-mail—to present concerns.

Model professionalism by letting go of past hurts.

Stay focused on our goals.

DECISION MAKING

Recognize that some decisions need to be made by the principal, such as approving budget expenditures, authorizing staff hires, and determining the effectiveness of employee performance.

Seek input from staff members regarding decisions that affect them.

Use nondivisive decision-making strategies (e.g., decision by consensus, surveys, and troubleshooting committees) and work out acceptable compromises.

SCHOOL OPERATIONS

Contribute to the effectiveness of staff meetings by arriving on time, listening attentively, avoiding side conversations, and sharing information in a *time-conscious* manner.

Keep the staff room a pleasant place by wiping up spills, bussing dishes, and sharing cleanup duties.

Observe schedules (e.g., arrive on time for events, vacate shared spaces punctually, and give notice of schedule changes).

Respect staff members' workspace and property (e.g., ask before taking, return items in good condition).

Show consideration for neighbors by keeping the volume down on AV equipment, moving students through shared areas *quietly*, and keeping family members—such as children—out of another's work space.

revised, and one they *dropped*. Be sure to ask for the thinking behind each decision. Then collect the results and craft a new version of the conduct norms. These revised expectations should be presented to staff for a final look at a subsequent meeting.

Once developed, bring your conduct code to life by using it to orient new staff members, mediate staff conflicts, or correct staff misconduct. You can also keep staff behavior on target by revisiting norms each fall and then again mid-year. Staff skits provide an engaging way to accomplish this review. Staff members act out code violations, such as talking negatively about colleagues, followed by scenes showing the professional way to observe behavior expectations.

Following the lead of savvy school counselors, actively using conduct norms in your school highlights *what* to do—an ideal way to strengthen everyone's professional behavior.

Provide Field Trip Guidelines

A principal called me after one of his primary teachers made a grievous error. While on a field trip to a large community park, the teacher lost track of several children who had scampered off in pursuit of butterflies. When it was time to head back to school, the kids were nowhere to be found. This frightening circumstance precipitated emergency calls to the police, the principal, the superintendent, and the children's parents followed by several hours of frantic searching. The children—and the teacher—were very lucky. The adventurous tykes were discovered unharmed and in good spirits. Nevertheless, the children's parents were irate and the superintendent was contemplating disciplinary action in regards to the ill-fated teacher.

As a first step, the superintendent asked the principal for verification that the teacher had been properly instructed regarding field trip supervision. Regrettably, the principal had nothing in writing that covered off-campus excursions. Field-trip expectations had not been covered in the teacher orientation packet, faculty bulletins, teacher meeting minutes, or the staff handbook. Worse than the lack of documentation, was the thought that this alarming incident might have been prevented had the teacher received proper guidance.

A reliable way to acquaint your teachers about field trip responsibilities is to provide them with written guidelines. You can handle this with an easy to use field trip checklist (Figure 3.4). Just make sure it aligns with district policies governing off campus activities, the use and training of chaperones, and student transportation guidelines. Your checklist should also cover the basics: getting principal approval, notifying food service and other affected departments, obtaining parent permission for student participation, and arranging for transportation and chaperones. Teachers should also be reminded to prepare for students with health, physical, cognitive, and behavior challenges.

To give emphasis to the Field Trip Checklist's importance, add it to your staff handbook and make its completion a field-trip requirement. With proper instruction, teachers will avoid mistakes that jeopardize the well-being of their students—and their careers.

Figure 3.4 Field Trip Checklist

Trip Date: Departure Time: Return Time: *Please Attach Itinerary*	Teachers Participating: Room Numbers: Classified Staff Participating:
Destination:	# of Students: *Please Attach List Prior to Departure*
Educational Purpose:	Names of Medically Fragile Students:
Transportation Mode: __Walking __Bus	# of Chaperones: *Please Attach List Prior to Departure*
Personal Cell #: Requesting School Cell Phone: __ Yes __ No	Destination Phone #:

Field trips should provide an educational experience for students and relate to instructional goals. They require preapproval from the principal and completion of the Field Trip Check List prior to departure.

Please (√) or write N/A for each item below:

- ☐ Request approval, via e-mail, from the principal—describe excursion and curriculum connection (1 month notice for walking trips, 2 months' notice for bus trips).
- ☐ Meet with the health attendant (24-hour notice, please) to make provisions for children with serious health conditions. It may not be appropriate to take medically fragile children off campus, for example, unless special arrangements are made and authorization is obtained from the district nurse.

(Figure continues on next page.)

☐ Pick up a first aid kit, the day before your trip, and obtain training from the health attendant regarding the administration of medications or Epi Pens.

☐ Notify the special education teachers if you have children with Individual Education Plans (IEPs) participating in the fieldtrip.

☐ Notify the cooks (1-week notice) and specialists so they are aware of your trip date and can revise their schedules and plans.

☐ Submit a Bus Request 2 months prior to the trip—see secretary for assistance. The secretary must call the transportation department 10 days in advance to reserve buses and notify dispatch of changes in time or destination. Please also specify if a special education minibus is required for a high-need child.

☐ Send home: field trip notice, itinerary, parent permission slip, and request for entry fees if appropriate (2-week notice). Every child must have a completed permission form to participate—only written permission on district-approved forms is accepted.

☐ Take the completed Parent Permission Forms with you on the trip. You may need family emergency information and phone numbers if a child requires emergency care.

☐ Collect fees according to district fiscal procedures—see the secretary for appropriate forms.

☐ Recruit sufficient chaperones for both bus and walking field trips. A ratio of 1 adult to 4 students for bus trips and 3 adults per class for walking trips is recommended, although a lower student-to-adult ratio may be required if there are safety hazards at the destination site. A child with special needs may also require 1-to-1 supervision.

☐ Check to see if the parents you have lined up to chaperone have completed appropriate application forms and have obtained the proper clearances.

☐ Check with secretary (2-week notice) for a purchase order for any required entry fees.

☐ Plan travel routes in advance (e.g., identify the safest pathways for students on walking field trips; locate appropriate parking locations for cars and busses on bus field trips).

☐ Request the school's cellular phone (1 day in advance) if you do not have your own.

☐ Don't lose your students! Monitor their whereabouts at all times and train chaperones how to properly supervise. Don't forget to count your students before you leave the school and prior to departing from your field trip location.

☐ Walking Field Trips: All steps, other than transportation, must be followed.

Date: ________ Teacher: ______________________________

Teach

I admire principals who are teachers of teachers. When you visit their schools you find them modeling instructional "best practices" in classrooms, orchestrating faculty discussions about teaching and learning, and sharing illuminating research from such fields as psychology, business, and science. The revitalized teachers of these exemplary leaders grow in competence.

School leaders would be missing a rich opportunity, however, if their teaching centered solely on pedagogy. Professionalism—the character, attitude, and behavior that one brings to the work place—is also a worthy topic. Unsurprisingly, professional development devoted to "professionalism" produces staff members who *act* more professionally.

A powerful way to nurture professionalism is through book studies. This approach sounds easy but there are six important steps to ensuring book study success:

Step 1: Choose a worthy book—one that fits your chosen theme, has substantive content, and is an easy read. The ideal book should be affordable, accessible, and run no more than a couple of hundred pages. I have the best success with book selection when I create an opportunity for teachers to peruse sample offerings at a staff meeting. I provide "sign up" sheets and when I get a minimum of ten staff members showing interest in a particular book, I choose it for a book study.

Step 2: Read the selected book in its entirety. You need to be completely comfortable with the philosophy, concepts, and skills advocated by the author. If you can't support key concepts choose another book.

Step 3: Decide who the participants will be—book studies can involve your entire faculty, a small teacher team, or a group of individuals who are self-selected. Consider inviting staff members from other schools—including secondary—to participate. Staff members from other schools and levels, such as middle school and high school, add interest to book study discussions.

Step 4: Announce your book study to a broad audience. An informative e-mail sent to every teacher in your school district is all it takes to get the ball rolling. Be sure to specify dates, times, and locations. Include information about where to obtain the book and an outline that identifies which chapters need to be read for each session. I have found that assigning just a couple of chapters per one hour meeting works well.

Step 5: Apply for college credit or "professional development hours." Book studies that help move teachers on the state salary schedule or meet certification renewal requirements will attract more teachers.

Step 6: Create support material such as "pop quizzes" and study guides. The quizzes (Figure 3.5) will encourage participants to read the book more attentively and the study guides (Figure 3.6, page 72) will help you facilitate meeting discussions.

Figure 3.5. Sample Pop Quiz

Book Study Pop Quiz

Todd Whitaker & Jeffery Zoul, *The 4 Core Factors for School Success* (Eye On Education, 2008): Chapter 1

DEFINITIONS

Core: ____(p. 5)

Actionable: ____(p. 7)

TRUE-FALSE

T F The ABCs identified by the authors are academics, benevolence, and Culture (p. 5).

T F The success of school improvement initiatives rests upon the successful the implementation of the 4 CORE Principles (p. 10).

FILL IN THE BLANK

To succeed as a professional educators, therefore, we must master the "people" skills of _____________ effectively, ____________ and monitoring carefully, building positive personal and professional ____________, establishing clear ______________ for ourselves, our students, and each other (p. 6).

We will expect our students to ___________, and we will __________ strategically and immediately when they are not (p. 9).

QUICK LIST

Jot down two actions for each of the following CORE principles (pp. 8–9):

Communication: ____

____

Observation: ____

____

Relationships: ____

____

Expectations: ____

____

Figure 3.6. Sample Book Study Guide

Book Study Guide

Todd Whitaker & Jeffery Zoul, *The 4 Core Factors for School Success* (Eye On Education, 2008): Chapter 1

Reflection Opportunity

The authors challenge educators to identify the "core principles on which we stand to guide us through times of change and conflict" (p. 4). What are *your* core principles?

____

____

____

What *actions* do you take to improve teaching and learning in your school?

____

____

____

Is it *people* or *programs* that make the most difference in schools? Why? Be prepared to explain your thinking.

____

____

____

Perfecting Professional Practice

List all the ways you communicate your school's mission. What actions could you add to strengthen communication with staff and clients?

____

____

____

What kinds of observations can you make in your school to assess instructional effectiveness? How would you use the information with students, teachers, and parents?

____

____

____

Do your staff members relate to each other in positive and constructive ways? If there are trouble spots, what steps could you take to strengthen relationships?

___

___

___

Some teachers are more effective than others in guiding and directing their students. What is it about these teachers' expectations that accounts for this difference? Compare the expectations of effective and ineffective teachers:

Effective Teachers	Ineffective Teachers
___	___
___	___
___	___

How could you help ineffective teachers become more effective?

___

___

___

Taking Action

Does your school have norms that guide staff member behavior? If your school has a behavior code, is it being observed? If not, ask your principal to create an opportunity for staff to review expectations. No norms? Then draft ideas for work place expectations and take them to your principal.

Many schools survey students regarding their attitudes towards school. The results may reveal problems in regards to staff–student relationships. Ask your counselor or student services director for the most current survey results and look for trouble spots. Share your analysis with your teacher team and principal.

Researching Resources

Looking for powerful ways to build school relationships? Todd Whitaker takes this on in *What Great Teachers Do* Differently*: Fourteen Things That Matter Most* (2004). This illuminating guide is available from Eye On Education (www.routledge.com).

As a book-study facilitator, your job is to record attendance, administer the pop quiz if you choose to use one, and lead participants through the chapter guides. Make sure you follow district and state regulations that govern professional development activities. In Washington State, for example, participants must accrue a minimum of three in-service hours to earn credits and must attend every training session.

Be prepared to liven things up if you have a reticent group—think of yourself as a social director. Draw out those reluctant to share; restrain those who tend to dominate the conversation, and interject a humorous comment or story. Make it fun!

If you are considering a book study about professionalism, you can't go wrong with either of the noteworthy books that follow:

- Todd Whitaker and Jeffery Zoul, *The 4 Core Factors for School Success* (Larchmont, NY: Eye On Education, 2008).

  Themes: This book shows how to communicate the school's mission, vision, and values; observe and monitor time, practices, and progress; build collaborative and supportive relationships; and convey clear expectations for self and others.

- Elaine K. McEwan, *10 Traits of Highly Effective Teachers: How to Hire, Coach, and Mentor Successful Teachers* (Thousand Oaks, CA: Corwin Press, 2002).

  Themes: The author identifies teacher traits—personal, teaching, and intellectual—that get results and contribute to the positiveness of the overall school culture.

The 4 Core Factors for School Success and the *10 Traits of Highly Effective Teachers* fit book selection criteria and promote exemplary behavior. Powerful books like these provide an ideal way to strengthen teacher competence and professionalism.

Intervene

Soon after becoming a principal I asked a well-respected superintendent to disclose his secrets to administrative success. After a reflective pause, the superintendent responded with these gems:

- Don't overspend your budget.
- Never cause your boss a sleepless night.
- And remember—if everybody likes you, you are *not* doing your job.

Initially I wasn't sure what to make of his *third* admonition. Aren't school leaders *supposed* to be likable? After a few months of employee supervision, however, its meaning became crystal clear. There are times when employee behavior—or the lack of—requires a supervisor's intervention. To no surprise, the supervisor may be perceived as unlikable, at least for a time. Nevertheless, responsible supervisors address staff misconduct regardless of the personal fallout. It may be uncomfortable but it is always the right thing to do.

When are interventions required? Consider these examples:

- Mr. Sienna, nicknamed "Burnt," is a busy teacher—*way* too busy to read all the rules and regulations that descend upon educators. So when Burnt gets the lengthy Classroom Safety Checklist distributed by Principal White, he tosses it. Consequently, Burnt fails to learn that cleaning chemicals brought from home may be hazardous and must be removed. Unauthorized cleaners, in fact, sit in full view on the counter by his classroom sink.
- Miss Vermillion loves art and over the years has acquired a wide range of equipment for her third grade classroom, including a small paper cutter that occupies a corner of her work table. Miss Vermillion isn't worried about the cutter injuring students, however. She has *repeatedly* reminded her curious third graders not to touch it.
- Miss Scarlet has two exits in her tiny classroom but blocks one with furniture because she never uses the exit and besides—she's desperate for wall space. What if there is an emergency requiring the use of the blocked exit? Not to worry! Miss Scarlet has a plan—she will *drag* the obstructing furniture out of the way.
- Miss Gold has several decades of teaching behind her and every year, she complains, the students get worse. "My class," she asserts, "is full of academic and behavior basket cases!" One day the principal overhears Miss Gold in the staff room tearing into Cobalt, a student she describes as "dysfunctional." His parents, Mr. and Mrs. Blue, are then characterized as "crazy." Miss Gold feels justified—it's only human to vent.
- Ms. Mauve is a night owl and getting to school on time, let alone faculty meetings, is a struggle. On staff meeting days Miss Mauve usually runs five to ten minutes late. One of Ms. Mauve's teaching colleagues, Miss Olive, takes notes for her

so Ms. Mauve isn't worried about her tardiness. She's got things covered.

Most school leaders would agree that the colorful cast of characters described in the foregoing scenarios need interventions—but how? What does an effective intervention look like? The answer depends on several variables: union contract language governing supervision, evaluation, and disciplinary action; school district personnel policies and procedures; and your intentions. If your objective is disciplinary action, for example, then proceed to the last tip in Theme 4 titled *Send for the Cavalry* as it outlines the initial steps. On the other hand, if you are merely after a speedy correction, then schedule a meeting with the staff member *after* consulting the pertinent union contract. There may be provisions that require written notice be provided *prior* to the meeting or that the employee be advised to bring a union representative. When in doubt, check with your human resources director or superintendent.

It may be, however, that formal notice and union representation are *only* necessary if you plan to cite the incident in an evaluation or use it as a springboard for disciplinary action. If neither is in your plans, then you can drop the formalities and proceed with a meeting. Many instances of staff misconduct are efficiently and effectively handled in this manner. Nevertheless, once the meeting has been held, send a followup memorandum to the employee that outlines the expectations you expressed.

What happens at the meeting? McEwan (2005) advises supervisors to script their comments ahead of time. This includes identifying the inappropriate behavior, describing the behavior that is expected, and explaining the rationale behind your request for a behavior change. By way of example, here is a sample script for the vignette featuring Miss Gold, the vituperative teacher who blasted little Cobalt and his parents, Mr. and Mrs. Blue. The principal's remarks were scripted ahead of time.

Principal White: Thank you for making time to see me. I requested this meeting because yesterday when I walked by the staff room I heard you describing Cobalt Blue, a student in your class, as "dysfunctional" and his parents as "crazy." I am concerned that you would talk about clients in the staff room and in this disrespectful manner.

Miss Gold: I just don't recall saying "dysfunctional" or "crazy." But I *do* remember being upset. Cobalt is impossible to deal with and his parents are maddening. I'm at my wits end!

Principal White: I can see that you are frustrated. Nevertheless, I expect you to stop talking about students and parents in the staff room. Otherwise you are violating school and district policies governing confidentiality. My second expectation is that you speak respectfully about the people you serve. Disrespectful comments are unprofessional and set a bad example for the rest of the staff. Both of these expectations are outlined in our school conduct code. [Hands copy to Miss Gold]

Miss Gold: I am not the *only* one who talks about students and parents in the staff room. There are others—I've heard some pretty vicious comments.

Principal White: Our focus today is what I heard *you* say yesterday. Your words and tone were disrespectful. I am directing you not to talk about clients in the staff room and not to speak disrespectfully about students and parents. Do you need any assistance in meeting these expectations? Seeing a counselor about your frustration, for example, is an option. Our employee support program provides counseling services at no charge.

Miss Gold: I don't need help; I just get a little hot under the collar sometimes. I'll follow the code.

In the foregoing scenario, Miss Gold was at first defensive and then later tried to shift blame to others. These are not unusual responses. Note that the principal stuck to his objectives, which included identifying the problem behavior, telling Miss Gold what was expected, and explaining why a shift in behavior was necessary. He also offered assistance which is always a good idea. However you script the meeting, the important thing is to say what you mean and mean what you say. Compliance is what you are after and with clear directives you will get it.

Suggested Readings

McEwan, Elaine K. (2005). *How to deal with teachers who are angry, troubled, exhausted, or just plain confused*. Thousand Oaks, CA: Corwin Press.

Smith, Richard E. (2009). *Human resources administration: A school-based perspective*, 4th ed. Larchmont, NY: Eye On Education.

Send for the Cavalry

Teachers cited for misconduct are like children who chronically misbehave—they believe in actions not words. These "misbehaving" adults ignore policies and procedures, fail to carry out directives, or act unprofessionally until someone puts a stop to it. In schools, it is the principal who is charged with stopping misconduct, and this is a serious and powerful responsibility.

Why do teachers misbehave? There are as many reasons as there are people. McEwan categorizes misbehaving teachers as "angry, troubled, exhausted, or just plain confused" (2005, p. xii). To this credible list I would add unethical, unorganized, and unmotivated. The *unethical* misuse sick leave, pilfer school supplies, or leave school without authorization. The *unorganized* fail to meet deadlines, complete required reports, or notify the office about major activities, such as taking kids off campus. The *unmotivated* are coasting; they do the bare minimum to get by and cut corners hoping no one will notice. The sad thing is that often no one does. Whatever the reasons, if a teacher generates significant or reoccurring problems, and fails to respond to interventions, disciplinary action may be warranted.

Disciplinary action includes warnings, reprimands, written reprimands, suspensions without pay, and even termination (Lawrence & Vachon, 2003). The first step on the disciplinary trail, however, is to send for the cavalry. This means notifying your human resources director and the superintendent. They, in turn, will alert your school district's attorney, if doing so becomes necessary.

In fairness to the teacher, suspicion of misconduct requires a thorough investigation. This begins with individual interviews that include the teacher and pertinent witnesses, such as other staff members or even students. Consult with your supervisors before initiating interviews, however. It might be best for the interviews to be conducted by someone other than you or, if there is suspicion that a crime has been committed, by law enforcement.

If *you* will be conducting the interviews appoint a note-taker, such as an administrative assistant or another principal. These notes should be summarized, typed, dated and signed by the note-taker and interviewer as the notes may become evidence if disciplinary action is taken.

Your next step is to assemble information pertinent to your case. This includes evidence of misconduct—investigative notes, records of prior interventions, and documentation that the teacher had been forewarned and properly trained. You will also need to prepare a brief that justifies the disciplinary action you are taking. This brief includes the description of the misconduct, including location, dates, and times; the impact upon students and/or staff; documentation of prior notice; expectations regarding attitude, behavior, and responsibilities; offers of assistance; and warning that future disciplinary actions will be taken if warranted. Don't panic—you don't need to be a legal whiz kid to get the job done. Your district-level supervisors are there to help you. They can even provide you with sample disciplinary action documents. The important thing is to pull essential information together in a logical, concise, and readable manner (Figure 3.7, page 80, provides an easy-to-follow example).

In regards to prior notice, here are the types of references that you can cite to verify that a teacher has been properly instructed:

- State Professional Standards
- Staff Conduct Code
- Position Description
- School Check-in Packet
- Staff Handbook
- Schedules
- Record of Staff Development
- Observation Reports
- Final and Interim Evaluations
- Intervention Memorandums
- Investigation Reports

Figure 3.7. Sample Disciplinary Action: Oral Reprimand

Date: {Month/Day/Year}

To: {Name of Teacher}, {Grade} Teacher

From: ______________________________, Principal

RE: ORAL REPRIMAND

This memorandum constitutes an Oral Reprimand and is in regards to the following concerns:

On {Date} you did not have lesson plans prepared for your substitute teacher. The school secretary had to call you at home so that you could verbally outline your plans for the substitute teacher. The following day I directed you to have written lesson plans for substitute teachers.

On {Date} you did not have lesson plans for your substitute teacher. I observed your grade-level colleagues assisting your substitute, {Name of Guest Teacher}, and providing her with instructional material. The substitute teacher reported that she could not find lesson plans or a Sub Handbook in your classroom or mailbox.

See attached Teacher/Guest Teacher Evaluation Form *for verification that lesson plans and a Sub Handbook were not provided.*

IMPACT

Failure to provide your substitute teachers with lesson plans and a current Sub Handbook has the following negative impacts: (1) students receive inadequate instruction; (2) the substitute teacher does not have the information needed to safeguard students, such as medical and behavior information; and (3) your colleagues are inconvenienced and their prep time compromised.

PRIOR NOTICE

- {Date} Verbal Reminder

  As noted above, you did not have written lesson plans on {date}. I reminded you to have written lesson plans for your guest teachers.

- {Year} Staff Handbook Expectation (p. 25):

  A Substitute Handbook (a template will be provided) should be prepared by teachers and specialists and a copy submitted to the office by the end of September. The original should be left in a permanent place in the classroom.

- {Year} Check-In Packet Expectation (pp. 4–5):

  ___ Draft lesson plans 3 days in advance in case of an emergency.

  ___ Provide subs with *written* plans—it is not permissible to phone them in. Complete the substitute evaluation form and return to the principal's mailbox.

Copies of two recent Check-In Packets are attached. You signed them {Date} and {Date}.

- {Year} E-mail Reminders

  The dean of students gave you three e-mail remainders in regards to completing the Sub Handbook. In addition, she placed your expired Sub Handbook in your mailbox with a note requesting completion of the current handbook.

  See e-mail from {Name}, dated {Date}, for months and specific dates.

EXPECTATIONS

Your failure to provide written lesson plans and a current Sub Handbook is *unsatisfactory*. You are directed provide substitute teachers with written lesson plans and an up to date Sub Handbook.

This expectation is supported by the State of Washington's *Code of Professional Conduct for Education Practitioners* (WAC 181–87–060: Disregard or Abandonment of Generally Recognized Professional Standards). The pertinent language reads:

> Any performance of professional practice in flagrant disregard or clear abandonment of generally recognized professional standards in the course of any of the following professional practices is an act of unprofessional conduct: (1) Assessment, treatment, instruction, or supervision of students...(*see attachment*).

The provision of "well organized series of learning opportunities and activities" for students is also outlined in the Granite Falls School District's position description for teachers. *See attached position description.*

ASSISTANCE

If you need help in regards to lesson format and content or with the preparation of the Sub Handbook, please ask myself or {Name}, Dean of Students, for assistance.

FUTURE ACTION

Your failure to observe previously clarified expectations in regards to lesson plans is *unsatisfactory*. You are directed to meet the directives spelled out in this memorandum (i.e., provide written lesson plans and an up-to-date Sub Handbook for the guest teachers who replace you). Failure to meet expectations may result in further disciplinary action, up to and including dismissal.

Attachments:

{Date} Certificated Staff Check-in Packet

{Date} E-mail to {Name} from {Name}

Teacher/Guest Teacher Evaluation Form: {Date}

Granite Falls School District Position Description

Code of Professional Conduct

Staff Handbook (p. 25)

Some school leaders avoid taking disciplinary action because they are fearful of the negative repercussions—from the employee, other staff members, or employee unions. Others are reluctant to spend the inordinate amount of time it takes to prepare their case and see it through. Although these reasons are understandable, neither justifies evading ones' responsibility. If you don't take action the behavior will continue and bring harm to students, staff, and the organization. When staff misconduct arises, taking action is *always* the right thing to do.

Suggested Readings

Lawrence, C. Edward, & Vachon, Myra K. (2003). *How to handle staff misconduct*, 2nd ed. Thousand Oaks, CA: Corwin Press.

Summing Up

- Be proactive—take steps to nurture professional staff behavior.
- Spell out job responsibilities in detail.
- Use check-in packets, field trip guidelines, handbooks, and other reference tools to delineate performance expectations.
- Create and actively use norms governing staff attitudes and behavior.
- Address behavior violations through intentional and explicit interventions.
- Teach professionalism.
- When chronic or severe misconduct arises—prepare to take action.

Making Connections

- How do you convey behavior expectations to your staff? Are there written references that staff members can go to for guidance? What documents, such as checklists, guidelines, and handbooks, do you need to fine-tune or prepare?
- Do you actively teach the concept of professionalism? How do your teachers learn about the character traits, attitudes, and behaviors associated with exemplary educators?

Strengthening Professional Practice

- Interview several colleagues who have taken disciplinary action in regards to staff misconduct, such as oral and written reprimands or a termination of employment. What steps did they take? What were the outcomes? What did these school leaders learn?
- Make a list of staff members in your school who have been failing to observe policies or procedures and are overdue for an intervention. Craft a script for one of these staff members and follow up with an intervention meeting. Did you gain compliance?

Theme 4

Mastering Emergency Management

Courage is being scared to death—but saddling up anyway.

— John Wayne (1907–1979)

Emergencies are like that well-worn quip about art—although tricky to define you know it when you see it. Like the time I watched a car pull onto my school's playground at recess time, slowly weaving in between and around clusters of highly mobile children, and then cruising to a stop alongside a classroom window. Inexplicably, the driver got out and yanked up the hood of his car. As I approached the driver to point out his less than stellar choice of a parking spot, his car's engine burst into spectacular flames! The startled driver panicked and the kids began shrieking hysterically. Despite the confusion, I quickly identified three objectives: keep the students away from the burning vehicle, get the fire put out, and calm the upset driver. Emergencies are like that car fire: they erupt without warning, require immediate action, and involve persons in urgent need of assistance (Merriam-Webster's, 2008).

What kinds of emergencies arise in schools? Crisis situations can be categorized by type and precipitant as demonstrated below:

Type of Emergency	Examples
Schoolwide emergencies	Fires Hazardous substances Power outages Large-scale plumbing failures
Natural disasters	Earthquakes Wind, snow, rain, ice storms Flooding Severe cold

Medical emergencies	Allergic reactions to food or insects Broken bones, head/neck injuries Diabetic complications Heart attacks Seizures Medication side effects or overdose Serious illness or death
Emergencies involving the police	Threatening intruders Parental custody disputes Out-of-control students, parents Student runaways

Regardless of the type of emergency, the response must be quick, efficient, and thorough. This requires prior training, skillful planning, ample practice, and effective teaming. Seem daunting? Relax. The tips offered in this section of the book teach you how to prepare in advance, activate a support team, and approach emergency situations competently and confidently.

Take Charge

When emergencies strike you have a leading role and your staff and students are counting on you to play it well. So no matter how anxious you might feel, be a good actor—project strength and confidence. This doesn't mean you should assume the flamboyant mannerisms and rapid fire delivery of Tommy Lee Jones, the actor who played the charismatic Director of Emergency Management in *Volcano*. When you take charge, a composed, soft-spoken demeanor will do as well. However you play the lead, your role entails activating emergency plans, directing the actions of students and staff, communicating with outside agencies, and keeping everyone calm and safe.

Solid crisis management begins with solid training. This includes learning about the job of the incident commander—the person who oversees the response to an emergency. A crisis handled solely at the school level puts the principal in this role. When outside agencies enter the picture, however, the incident command position usually shifts to an official from the fire or police department. In some states, school administrators are required to complete coursework that introduces them to the incident command system. This crucial training is available online from the Emergency Management Institute, a division of the Federal Emergency Management Agency.

Is your school district part of a web-based crisis management system, such as *Rapid Responder*? This online emergency system provides outside agencies instant access to school contact information, facility maps, floor plans, photos, and lists of potential hazards. If your school is involved in an online system like this, training in how to use and update your school's profile is a must.

Other training that school leaders need include the following:

Emergency preparedness	Identifying and assembling emergency supplies and equipment. Creating and practicing response procedures.
Drill management	Teaching students and staff how to respond to the following emergencies: ♦ Earthquake ♦ Fire ♦ Hazardous Substances ♦ Lock Down
Health	Learning how to give first aid and CPR; use a defibrillator; and control the spread of infectious diseases.
Deescalation	Defusing "acting-out" students. Calming angry adults.
Restraint	Acquiring safe techniques for holding or moving students who are a danger to themselves or to others.

After you identify what you need in the way of training, contact the people who can help you get it. This includes your superintendent, human resources director, and your professional association's in-service director.

While you are waiting to get up to speed, don't forget to connect with experienced school principals who are leading schools in your area. These veterans will gladly share their crisis plans, demonstrate emergency procedures, and help you troubleshoot problems. Meanwhile, think about the role you will play the next time you hold a drill or manage an emergency. Remember to project strength and confidence and then "take charge."

Suggested Readings

Introduction to the Incident Command System (ICS-100.a). http://training.fema.gov/EMIWeb/ IS/IS100a.asp

Center for Education & Employment Law. (2009). *Keeping your school safe & secure: A practical guide,* Third Edition. Malvern, PA: Author.

Simplify

When I wrote my first "threatening intruder" plan, I called upon community experts for help—the local chief of police and the manager of the town bank. These security pros taught me the essentials then gave me a solid tip: keep the response plan simple. With this tip in mind, I used a bullet format and kept narratives to a minimum (Figure 4.1). My staff appreciated that procedures, role descriptions, and alert signals were easy to locate and understand. I maintained the "less-is-more" approach when I developed additional crisis plans for my school's Emergency Handbook.

What emergencies should you prepare for? Examples follow; note that they are listed in alphabetical order, the same "easy-to-find" order they should appear in your emergency handbook.

Adverse Weather Conditions
Bomb Threat
Bus Accidents
Death of Student or Staff Member
Earthquake
Fire
Hazardous Substances
Medical Emergency (911 Call)
Power Outage
Suicide Threat
Terrorist Attack
Threatening Intruder
Violent Student

In addition to the aforementioned plans, a comprehensive emergency guide includes an outline of the principal's basic responsibilities. These tasks, which will apply to most but not all emergencies, include gathering facts, notifying key people, planning the response, keeping staff informed, and debriefing staff and response team members (see Figure 1.6, page 24). Other useful handbook additions include staff roles and responsibilities; your school's chain of command—who takes over in the principal's absence; the membership of response teams, such as Search and Rescue; student and staff rosters; alternate relocation plans; facility maps; the location of electrical panels and gas and water turnoff valves; and emergency phone numbers.

(Text continues on page 91.)

Figure 4.1. Threatening Intruder Response Plan

Lockdown Procedures

A threatening intruder, as defined in this document, is an individual who has a visible weapon (e.g., gun, knife, explosive) or who is suspected—because of words or actions—of having a concealed weapon.

Emergency Alerts

Lockdown procedures will be implemented in response to an emergency alert or when a disturbing sound (e.g., gun fire, an explosion) is heard.

Disturbing Sound	=	Gun fire, explosion
Intercom Announcement	=	Lockdown, Lockdown, Lockdown
Message Delivered to Room	=	Lockdown

Lockdown Procedures

- Check hall quickly for passing students and direct them into classrooms.
- Lock door (do not open once door is locked).
- Cover window on door.
- Close blinds (do not open once closed).
- Turn out lights.
- Instruct students to sit on the floor with you—away from the door or windows; remain silent, but if you hear gunfire direct students to take cover.
- Wait for further instructions (e.g., all-clear signal)

If in the hall, gym, or cafeteria:

- Go to the nearest room with space available and follow lockdown procedures,

  or
- Run out nearest exit to an off-campus site (e.g., district office).

If outdoors:

- Using your best judgment, direct students to reenter the school building, crouch down, take cover behind equipment, or to run (e.g., toward the gate leading to town).
- If you choose to run from the school grounds, lead students to an off-campus site (e.g., middle school).

Staff members will, in response to emergency alerts:

- Implement lockdown procedures.

(Figure continues on next page.)

Staff members will, when observing a threatening intruder from a distance:

- Do not alert the intruder that he or she has been seen.
- Notify police (911) on nearest phone and stay on the line.
- Describe the intruder, his/her location and behavior, and weapon.
- Notify office staff (e.g., send someone to call on another phone).
- Notify other personnel *if safe* to do so (e.g., send a "Lockdown" message)

Staff members will, when face to face with a threatening intruder:

- Attempt to remain at a safe distance.
- Remain calm.
- Act in a nonthreatening manner.
- Ask the intruder to report to the office (if the intruder leaves you, get to the nearest phone and alert the office staff, then call 911).
- Always tell the intruder what you plan to do before you do it.
- If it appears safe to do so, direct students to another location.
- Use appropriate hand signs (1 finger = OK; 2 fingers = stay close; 3 fingers = get help; fist = weapon observed) to alert other staff.
- Engage the intruder in a conversation; keep him/her occupied and calm.
- If an intruder enters your room with a weapon, instruct students to sit quietly or to take cover—whichever seems most appropriate given the behavior of the intruder.

The office staff will, when confronted by a threatening intruder:

- Stay calm and engage the intruder in conversation.
- Act in a nonthreatening manner.
- Notify intruder of plans (e.g., don't use intercom without permission).
- If safe to do so, notify police (call 911).
- Use your best judgment regarding requests from the intruder.
- If the intruder abducts a student, get a description of the vehicle and exit route.
- If a student or staff member is harmed, ask for permission to give first aid.
- Call emergency medical personnel when safe to do so.
- Notify superintendent when safe to do so.
- Post signs for parents at the front doors if appropriate; advise parents to listen to regional news stations or access the district website for updates

The District Office Response Team will:

- Arrange for streets and the school parking lots to be blocked from traffic.
- Liaison with police and fire departments.
- Handle media coverage.

After the Emergency Is Over

The teachers will:

- Keep children in classrooms or a designated area.
- Release students only when authorized to do so by office staff.

The Code Blue Team will:

- Assist teachers with students.
- Assist the principal, secretary, and emergency personnel.
- Meet with the principal to develop a response plan.

The principal and secretaries will:

- Follow pertinent procedures outlined in the *Principal's Checklist.*
- Establish a student signout procedure and location.

The counselor will:

- Provide comfort and support to students and staff.
- Assist the principal and office staff as needed.
- Follow procedures outlined in the *Principal's Checklist.*

I keep my Emergency Handbook in an easy-to-tote canvas bag along with emergency equipment and supplies, such as orange vests, whistles, a first aid kit, flashlights, and writing pads and pens. This well-stocked kit comes in handy during drills, school evacuations, and other school emergencies. Whatever the situation, the first tool I grab is the Emergency Handbook—the substantive yet simplified directions are a lifesaver.

Use Protocols

The health rooms in our school district are run by a cadre of dedicated health attendants with hearts as big as the earth and a knack for bringing aid and comfort to the injured and ill. These attendants are not licensed health professionals, however, so they are trained and supervised by a highly skilled registered nurse. Many of our students have serious medical problems and when complications arise, proper care can mean the difference between life and death. To prevent mistakes, our registered nurse prepares "protocols" for the health attendants to follow. These protocols are concise, step-by-step treatment plans that help insure that her instructions, and those of physicians, are followed to the letter.

I borrowed the protocol concept when developing response plans for short-term school emergencies, such as 911 Medical Calls, students who come up missing at school (Figure 4.2, page 94), bus riders who fail to reach their destinations, and modified lockdowns. I wanted a reference my secretaries and I could grab in a hurry, follow easily, and feel confident using. Our protocols differ from the plans in our Emergency Handbook in a couple of ways: they are written specifically for the office staff and cover emergency essentials without unnecessary details. An example of a modified lockdown protocol is shown on the next page.

We keep emergency protocols in a desktop document organizer because the pages easily flip from one to the next. The plastic pockets that house the documents have color-coded frames—we use red for emergency protocols—and metal prongs that easily slip in and out of the organizer's base. We can quickly pull the protocols we need and easily replace them once the emergency is over. Protocols are the perfect tools for short-term, unexpected, but serious emergencies. Use them.

Activate a Support Team

"We need help," I whispered, as I knelt alongside a school volunteer who had just been hit by a car. I was speaking to my health attendant smack dab in the middle of my school's parking lot at the height of a hectic dismissal time. We needed help alright and lots of it: cars needed to be routed away from the scene of the accident, parking spots found for arriving police and fire department vehicles, the scene cordoned off, and bystanders kept away. Someone also needed to get the names of everyone involved in the accident and liaison with the police, fire department, and the victim's family. Leaving the victim in my health attendant's expert care, I rounded up staff members to assist with the most urgent tasks and soon had the situation under control. But later when I had time to reflect, I knew I wanted something better. When an emergency arose, I didn't want to go searching for help—I wanted help to come to me. So I set up a team that I activate when a medical emergency arises (Figure 4.3, page 95). The team is called Code Blue—the signal hospitals use to announce that an emergency is in progress, such as a patient in cardiac arrest. The Code Blue team is comprised of staff members who are not assigned to classrooms and includes the counselor, librarian, reading teacher, and various specialists. The duties of the Code Blue team members include the following:

- Assisting the principal and office staff with emergency protocol tasks.

(Text continues on page 96.)

Modified Lockdown

When to Activate:

At the request of police because of activity near the school, upon receiving reports of potential threatening intruders, or when off-campus persons or activities that may pose a threat are observed.

Principal:

- ☐ Tell custodian to secure every exit door
- ☐ Send e-mail titled "Principal Update" that announces the modified lockdown:

  The school is in a modified lockdown because of police activity

  Lock exterior classroom doors (*do not* lock interior doors)

  Take roll and report missing students to office staff

  Keep indoors—recesses will be held in classrooms

  Carry on with normal routine, including going to PE, music, and library

  Classes held in the portables have been relocated to *{specify locations}*
- ☐ Intercom staff to check e-mail for a message titled "Principal Update"
- ☐ Arrange for in-class recesses (assign supervisors)
- ☐ Notify staff when the modified lockdown is over

Secretaries:

- ☐ Notify police
- ☐ Radio student supervisors to bring in students from recess
- ☐ Notify staff in portables to move into the main building
- ☐ Put sign on door:

  Modified lockdown in progress. Police activity in the area. No entry granted. Check the school district website, your e-mail, or local news sources for details.
- ☐ Notify the superintendent
- ☐ Notify substitute teachers who do not have e-mail access
- ☐ Notify superintendent when the modified lockdown is over
- ☐ If students are interviewed by police, notify parents.

Figure 4.2. Protocol: Missing Student

Search Start Time: ____________ End Time: ____________

Teacher

- Notifies the office staff that a student is missing
- Identifies where and when last seen
- Describes clothing and appearance
- Names other staff the student works with
- Names close friends of the student
- Helps with the search if coverage can be provided for the teacher's classroom

Office Staff

- Records time teacher notification is received
- Intercom All Call: Requests missing student to report to the office
- Radios playground supervisors to search the playground
- Checks student "pickup list"
- Looks up address, phone number, and photo of student
- If student not found, notify police (911) within 10 minutes, parents, district office

  Time Police Called: ___________ Time Police Arrived: ___________

Principal

- Reports to the office upon hearing the All Call
- Assigns staff members to search bathrooms and wings A, B, and C
- Assigns a staff member to search playground "hiding places" (e.g., tires)
- Determines when to notify the police and parents (Time Limit Guide: 10 minutes)

Figure 4.3. Protocol: 911 Call for Medical Emergencies

Office Staff

The office staff will:

- Call 911 (describe situation)
- Notify health attendant, principal or designee, and office staff
- Send health attendant to victim
- Send first aid kit, 2-way radio, defibrillator (if victim unconscious)
- Call Code Blue Team to report to *(specify location)*
- Call district nurse *(telephone and/or extension number)*
- Contact victim's family
- Notify the district office of the 911 call *(telephone and/or extension number)*
- Make two sets of the following (one for emergency responders; one for principal):
  - Health Information Form
  - Emergency Authorization Form
  - Medical Release Form
  - Physician's Orders & Care Plan
  - Emergency Contact Information

Principal

Assign Code Blue Team members to:

- Clear emergency area of unnecessary persons
- Control parking lot traffic
- Greet medics and escort to victim
- If in the office:
  - Block entrances to office area
  - Move visitor sign in station to the hallway
  - Close doors to the cafeteria and gym
  - Prevent unnecessary persons from entering the door to the health room
  - Liaison with emergency responders
- Follow aid car to hospital; take school cell phone and the following:
  - Health Information Form
  - Emergency Authorization Form
  - Medical Release Form
  - Physician's Orders & Care Plan
  - Emergency Contact Information
- After the emergency is over, send an e-mail to staff notifying them of the incident and a letter to the parents of students who witnessed the emergency
- Debrief crisis response team within 24 hours

- Keeping students, staff, and bystanders away from the location of the emergency.
- Greeting the fire department's aid car and escorting medical personnel to the victim.
- Directing bus, parking lot, and foot traffic.
- Assuming other duties assigned by the principal, such as serving as media spokesperson, meeting recorder, or liaison with the victim's family.
- Developing postemergency communications for students, parents, and staff.
- Assisting the principal with the implementation of preplanned emergency drills.

The Code Blue team is activated by an intercom announcement: "Code Blue Team report to (*location of emergency*)." Since the team has been in effect, emergency locations have included the office, gym, playground, bus loading area, and various classrooms and hallways. Team members with students at the time of the "All Call" send them back to their classroom teachers. When team members are no longer needed, they resume their regular duties. I can't imagine handling an emergency without the help of a Code Blue team; can you? If not, then put your team together today.

Practice, Practice, Practice

Awhile back I was the principal of a large elementary school that caught fire during the middle of a school day. When the alarm sounded, two-thirds of the school's 500 students were assembled in the gym watching a play; the remaining students were at work in their classrooms in the wing where the fire started. Fortunately, the evacuation of the students went smoothly and no child turned up missing. As fortuitous was the instantaneous response of the local fire department—the blaze was doused within eight minutes of the initial alarm. This bravura performance did not happen by chance; between calls at the station house firefighters practice fire suppression, search and rescue, and first aid procedures until they become second nature. Smart school leaders take this same approach to emergency preparedness—they get everyone practicing.

There are four emergency drills that should be rehearsed regularly: earthquake, fire, hazardous substance, and lockdown. Teachers should teach their students the procedures for each type of drill within the first month of school. After this initial training, "all school" drills are generally scheduled monthly on a rotating basis. Be sure to check your district policy and state regulations, however, regarding drill requirements. Scheduling six fire drills a year is a must in my state and one needs to occur during an assembly. Given my experience with school fires, the assembly fire drill is the first one I hold.

When it is time to conduct a drill the checklist that follows will help you and others prepare:

Drill Preparation Check-list

- ☐ Notify office staff and school nurse
- ☐ Notify head custodian to sound alarm at specified time
- ☐ Notify substitute teachers to review drill plans
- ☐ Fall only: Notify preschool and kindergarten teachers to prepare students
- ☐ Fall only: Notify teachers with medically fragile children to prepare students
- ☐ Notify district office secretary: *{Phone Number}*
- ☐ Notify police department: *{Phone Number}*
- ☐ Notify fire department: *{Phone Number}*
- ☐ Notify the school's security alarm company *before* drill: {Phone Number}
- ☐ Hang the Emergency Drill Notice sign on the front entrance door
- ☐ Notify the school's security alarm company *after* the drill: *{Phone Number}*
- ☐ Complete an emergency drill report and send copy to the superintendent.

Note that prior to the fall drills, I give a heads-up to teachers with very young or medically fragile children. I want these sensitive youngsters forewarned so that they are not frightened by unexpected sounds and actions. This prenotification is no longer necessary after the students get a few drills under their belts.

When a drill or emergency requires an evacuation, checking for missing students and staff members is top priority. This needs to be done efficiently so that arriving emergency personnel can begin searching for persons still inside the school. I have a large student body and faculty, so I use a combination of strategies to identify missing persons quickly. These are outlined below:

Green and red teacher signs	After taking roll, each teacher holds the appropriately colored sign aloft: Green = all students present; Red = missing or extra student to report.

Line checkers	Checks in with teachers holding red signs and records the names of missing or extra students then reports the information to the principal via two-way radios. Students with specialists are also recorded and reported to the principal.
Cross referencing	The principal and office staff "cross reference" the names of missing students against the reports of extra students and students with specialists. Names are also checked against the office log of students picked up early from school. Any student or staff member not accounted for is reported to the fire department incident commander.

In addition to procedure practice, drills provide opportunities to check on emergency equipment. Will the alarm system activate when a fire box is pulled? Will the alarm control panel indicate *where* in the building an alarm was set off? Are two-way radios operable? Will automatic fire doors close? Your custodial staff should always check on the reliability of emergency equipment during drills and report malfunctions.

Staff members need to know their roles during an emergency and these should be delineated in the Emergency Handbook. The response plan for school fires (Figure 4.4) provides an example. There are detailed instructions for staff members, the office staff, health attendant, custodian, the Code Blue team, and the principal. Note the specificity of the instructions—the school secretaries, for example, know that they are to call the fire department, evacuate students in their area, take out the volunteer and student sign in/out logs, cell phone, two-way radios, and the rolling cart that is filled with emergency equipment and supplies.

Figure 4.4. School Fire Response Plan

Staff members will, when encountering a fire:

- Pull nearest alarm.
- Evacuate students out nearest exit, use alternative route if needed.
- Report location of fire to office staff.

The office staff upon hearing a fire alarm will:

- Evacuate students in office area.
- Call fire department (911).
- Take out: cell phone, two-way radios, volunteer & student checkout logs, notepads and pencils, rolling emergency cart, and other pertinent materials.

The class line checkers will:

- Obtain two-way radios, if possible.
- Report to principal for assignment.
- Check designated classroom lines & note missing students.
- Report results to principal.

Staff members will:

- Evacuate building in a controlled manner.
- Use alternate exit route as needed.
- Walk students—who should be silent—to line up location.
- Special education, WRC, Title I, and office staff: Send students back to homeroom teachers (unless assigned to the nurse because of illness)
- Take headcount or roll.
- Hold up a green sign if you have nothing to report; hold up a red sign if you *do* have something to report.
- Report missing students or extra students and their locations.
- Reenter building only if instructed to do so.
- Wait silently for further instructions.

The custodian will:

- Check restrooms for students
- Check location of alarm.
- Notify principal & fire department of fire location.

Code Blue Team members will:

- Report to the principal to offer assistance.
- Carry out assigned duties, such as checking lines for missing or extra students.
- Assist the principal with emergency activities.

(Figure continues on next page.)

The principal will:

- Ensure that the location of the fire has been reported to fire department personnel.
- Identify missing students and staff and relay information to the fire department's incident commander.
- Follow procedures in the *Principal's Checklist*.
- Keep staff informed of developments.
- Relocate students and staff to an alternate site, if necessary.
- Notify superintendent.

If you have a school fire, will everyone know their part? They will if you start with a solid response plan and then practice, practice, practice.

Set Student Expectations

It was ten minutes to dismissal time when a construction worker from an adjacent building site burst into the school office with startling news: "We've got dynamite set to detonate and my boss thinks there might be too much." "So what happens if your boss is right?" I asked steadily. "In about five minutes," he calmly replied, all your windows will blow out. By "windows" he was referring to the pairs of gigantic, double paned, picture windows that graced every classroom.

With no time to debate the hair-raising possibility of flying window panes, my secretary and I cooked up a plan. We would have an earthquake drill in the hallways! We scurried from classroom to classroom room announcing this zany news, which gave rise to more than a few teacher's eyebrows and brought student looks that read: "Is this for real?" When the last class settled into place—kids and teachers crouched in silence along interior hallway walls—a tremendous explosion shook the building to its core. I learned later that every window had flexed dramatically in and out before coming to rest still intact in its frame.

I was glad the windows survived, but as importantly that the impromptu earthquake drill was executed so swiftly and proficiently by our students. Isn't that the true test of any emergency plan? The students performed admirably because they had been taught the role *they* play during emergencies (Figure 4.5). The following student behavior should be nonnegotiable:

Student Emergency Expectations

Be Silent

Walk

Listen

Follow Directions

Figure 4.5. Student and Staff Roles During Emergency Evacuations

Student Roles

- Be silent—silence is lifesaving.
- Walk in an orderly, single file line.
- Listen for directions—your exit route or line up location may have to be changed.
- Follow directions given by your teacher, other supervisors, and emergency personnel.

Certificated Staff Roles

- Evacuate students using the nearest, safe exit route.
- Take your emergency kit, personal cell phone, purse or wallet, and car keys.
- Line up students in designated location—unless unsafe to do so.
- Check for missing students by taking roll.
- Hold up a *green* sign if you have nothing to report and a *red* sign if you do.
- Report missing or extra students and any illnesses or injuries to the drill "line checker."
- Report injured or ill students.
- Keep students silent and orderly until the drill or emergency is over.

Classified Staff

- Evacuate students under your supervision.
- Escort students to the appropriate teacher lines.
- Assist certificated staff with students.
- Respond to calls for assistance from the principal.

Custodian

- Liaison with arriving emergency personnel—fire, police, etc.
- Check the operation of the alarm system and fire doors during fire drills.
- Keep in contact with the principal via two-way radio.

Secretaries

- Report emergency: call 911 if necessary.
- Follow emergency handbook and protocol procedures.
- Notify superintendent's office staff of the emergency.
- Take out emergency kit, enrollment book, volunteer/visitor log, student checkout log, contact information, two-way radios, cell phone.
- Set up a "student release" station in an appropriate location if necessary.
- Keep in contact with the principal.

(Figure continues on next page.)

Health Attendant

- Evacuate sick or injured students.
- Take emergency, first aid, and defibrillator kits.
- Set up a first aid station and provide first aid as needed.
- Refer injured and ill students to arriving medical personnel.

Why the silence? Students are less likely to panic. They will also hear their teacher's directions should circumstances require a deviation from the usual procedures. Such was the case during the school fire described in the preceding chapter. Students in the wing where the fire started had to be directed to alternative exit routes, the kids at the assembly needed instructions regarding the best doors to depart from, and several class groups that had assembled outside the school required relocation because they were too near firefighting equipment.

When students live up to drill expectations, heap on the praise. I do that with personal notes and "teamwork tickets." These much sought after tickets are cashed in for incentives, such as extra recesses, pizza parties, or entertaining but educational movies. What happens if students fail to live up to expectations? They practice until they get it right.

The expectations you set—or fail to set—will determine whether or not students are kept safe and contribute to the safety of others. Your students will rise to the occasion in any emergency if you provide ample practice and praise.

Summing Up

- No matter how anxious you might feel during an emergency, project strength and confidence.
- Get the training you need to manage emergencies confidently and competently.
- Prepare comprehensive emergency plans but keep them simple.
- Emergency protocols are your recipe for success.
- Take a team approach to crisis management.
- Practice makes perfect.
- Set high expectations for students during emergencies and drills.

Making Connections

- How do you handle emergency drills and authentic emergencies? What persona do you play? Is it effective? Why or why not?
- Think about your last emergency drill. If you were to give it a letter grade would it be an A+? Why or why not? What will you do next time to insure a quality performance?

Strengthening Professional Practice

- Create a professional development plan for emergency preparedness and management. Include training sources and timelines.
- Review your emergency plans. Are they easy to read? How can you revise the format and wording to make them a breeze to understand and implement?

Theme 5

Breaking Through Success Barriers

Vision is the driving force that communicates an instructional leader's image of the future and is based on personal values, beliefs, and experiences. A vision stretches the imagination and requires the ability to see the future in a way that others may not.

— McEwan (2009, p. 55)

I have been principal of nine elementary schools—not counting the one-room schoolhouse that was once under my care. I found each school to be unique, varying according to student demographics, such as the percentage of special education students, children in poverty, and English language learners; the socioeconomic status of the community; teacher training and experience; school climate and culture; student progress as measured by district and state achievement tests; and school strengths, such as strong parent participation. Some schools were particularly intriguing because they were polar opposites. One elementary, for example, served affluent, highly educated families from a homogenous neighborhood adjacent to a university. In contrast, its "opposite" was in an agricultural community and drew children from neighborhoods characterized by high poverty, multiple languages, and diverse ethnic cultures.

Despite the differences among the nine schools, there was a shared characteristic—all needed to strengthen student performance. Even in schools where student test scores were high there were pockets of problems, such as males falling behind females in writing or special education students failing to make gains in math. Over time I learned that no matter the makeup of the school, the achievement strengths or challenges, or the barriers to student success, it was *my* job as school leader to get my teachers behind improving student learning.

Raising student achievement is an exacting adventure that requires *every* staff member's instructional expertise, creative energy, and enthusiastic participation. This is a collective enterprise—no holdouts allowed. Consequently, the first step in improving student learning is "finding ways to develop a sense of clarity and coherent support for improving instruction" (Copland & Knapp, 2006, p. 87). Copland and Knapp (2006) inform us that coherence brings an alignment of effort among staff members, a shared vision, and a strong commitment to improving student learning. Worthy goals but how do school leaders attain them?

Theme 5 presents structures and processes that help teachers understand the power of "coherence." Tips include how to craft a Theory of Action and supporting strategies, develop effective action plans, use data strategically, and strengthen staff alignment and performance.

Develop a Theory of Action

I love to bake scones—those triangular Scottish pastries that are a coffeehouse favorite. My ideal scone has a tender, flaky interior; a rich, buttery taste; and a golden brown, crisp crust. When scones are served hot from the oven with homemade jam and fresh-brewed coffee, I have reached the promised land. How do you get the perfect scone? There are numerous theories on the subject and countless recipes. Fortunately, after considerable research and experimentation, I learned how to create the quintessential scone. My formula for success is based upon a concept called Theory of Action—an "if–then" proposition that identifies the cause-and-effect relationship between *actions* taken and *outcomes* (Copland, 2009). In regards to scones, the if–then propositions look like this:

- *If* buttermilk is used instead of regular milk, *then* the scones will be crisper and crunchier.
- *If* the eggs, butter, and buttermilk are kept ice box cold, *then* the scones will be flakier.
- *If* baking soda is added to the baking powder, *then* the scones will rise higher and be more tender.

In the academic world, a Theory of Action identifies critical actions that teachers can employ to boost student achievement. By way of examples, here are a couple of Theory of Action proposals for improving student performance in reading:

Theory of Actions for Reading

- *If* teachers implement a research based reading program that aligns to state standards, spirals from grade to grade, and includes oral reading fluency practice, *then* students' reading achievement will rise.
- *If* teachers provide reading material at students' instructional levels, schedule fluency practice, use fluency progress monitoring assessments, and help students chart their own progress, *then* students' oral reading fluency will increase.

A Theory of Action for improving student learning may be proven *valid* if the desired results are achieved or *invalid* if the results are *not* attained (City et al., 2009). The important thing is to keep tinkering with instructional interventions—just like I did with my recipe for scones—until you get what you are after. In the case of reading, desired outcomes include a rise in students' instructional levels, an increase in oral reading fluency scores, more kids passing summative reading tests, and a higher percentage of students meeting state reading benchmarks

The Theory of Action concept came in handy when I became concerned about my students' computational fluency. After seven years of a constructivist math program, one that had been highly recommended at the state level, our students were picking up math concepts but floundering with respect to math computation skills. Skills that our state was *now* emphasizing as important in a well-rounded math program. We knew our math curriculum was computationally weak but to find out *exactly* where our students stood we administered a computational fluency test from AIMSweb, an academic progress monitoring system. Our results were worse than we had anticipated. Only 25% of students in grades 1 through 5 were at benchmark for computational fluency, and a whopping 54% were in the intensive category.

With the help of my staff, we implemented the Theory of Action concept using the activity described in Figure 5.1 (page 108). The teachers and support specialists, working in grade-level and department groups, generated powerful ideas for our Theory of Action. After some minor editing on my part, it looked like this:

Theory of Action for Computational Fluency

> *If* teachers provide uniformity in regards to instruction and student performance expectations, align computation curriculum with state standards, provide computational fluency practice, and use student performance data to drive instruction, *then* students' computational fluency will improve.

Crafting a Theory of Action had many benefits. The if–then proposition clarified for teachers the critical attributes of our computational fluency mission. This included providing cohesive instruction, aligning curriculum to standards, and scheduling and monitoring fluency practice. It also gave us a framework for developing the specific classroom based actions described in the following section, *Keep Tinkering*.

Figure 5.1. Theory of Action Staff Meeting

Format: Grade-Level & Specialist Team Groups

Purpose: To develop a Theory of Action for computational fluency. A Theory of Action is an if–then proposition that reveals a cause-and-effect relationship between actions taken and the outcome (Copeland, 2009).

Examples: Theory of Actions for Reading

- ***If*** teachers implement a research based reading program that aligns to state standards, spirals from grade to grade, and includes oral reading fluency practice, ***then*** students' reading achievement will rise.
- ***If*** teachers provide reading material at students' instructional levels, schedule fluency practice, use fluency progress monitoring assessments, and help students chart their own progress, ***then*** students' oral reading fluency will increase.

Group Facilitator: The staff member who has taught the most years at our school.

Recorder/Reporter: The staff member who has taught the fewest years.

Step 1 Review the fall computational fluency data. What are our strengths? What needs to be strengthened?

____

____

____

Step 2 What should be our theory of action for computational fluency?

If teachers…

____

____

____

____

____

then students' computational fluency will increase.

Keep Tinkering

Writing a Theory of Action to improve student performance is a solid idea. In just a few lines, core beliefs are succinctly captured, as was the case with our Theory of Action for computational fluency:

Theory of Action for Computational Fluency

> ***If*** teachers provide uniformity in regards to instruction and student performance expectations, align computation curriculum with state standards, provide computational fluency practice, and use student performance data to drive instruction, ***then*** students' computational fluency will improve.

A thoughtfully developed Theory of Action provides staff with immediate direction and serves as a sign post to guide future actions. The Theory of Action's success or failure, however, rests upon the specific strategies employed by teachers at the classroom level. As Fullan puts it so nicely: "a good theory explains not how you *want* the world to work, but how it *actually* works" (2008, p. 125). Ideas for strategies, which should be identified collaboratively by principal and teachers, will spring from staff member's experience, training, and research regarding best practices. In regards to oral reading fluency, for example, my thoughtful staff generated a variety of effective strategies (Figure 5.2, page 110) such as daily fluency practice, monitoring progress, and charting student growth. Student performance improved; during the 2009–2010 school year, for example, all but one grade level made reading fluency gains:

	Fall (%)	Spring (%)	Gains (%)
Kindergarten	49	63	+14
Grade 1	63	83	+20
Grade 2	72	73	+01
Grade 3	64	64	00
Grade 4	73	84	+11
Grade 5	68	74	+06

The increase in first grade was especially noteworthy; 63% of the students entered the fall of 2009 at benchmark for oral reading fluency but nine months later, 83% of these students met standards.

Figure 5.2. Theory of Action and Strategies for Oral Reading Fluency

If teachers provide reading material at students' instructional levels, schedule fluency practice, use fluency progress monitoring assessments, and help students chart their own progress, ***then*** students' oral reading fluency will increase.

Kindergarten	1st Grade	2nd Grade	3rd Grade	4th Grade	5th Grade
Practice oral reading fluency daily		Practice oral reading fluency 3–5 times a week	Practice oral reading fluency daily	Practice oral reading fluency 3–5 times a week	Practice oral reading fluency daily
Read letters, sight words, fluency passages, books	Read sight words, fluency passages, decodable books, books, Open Court anthology stories		Read fluency passages, chapter books, Open Court anthology stories	Read fluency passages, Imagine It anthology stories, text from online sources	Read poetry, plays, Imagine It anthology stories books

<table>
<tr><th>Kindergarten</th><th>1st Grade</th><th>2nd Grade</th><th>3rd Grade</th><th>4th Grade</th><th>5th Grade</th></tr>
<tr><td>Track progress in a notebook and by using the fluency database reports</td><td colspan="5">Track progress using “cold” and “hot” timings, by charting progress, and using the fluency database reports</td></tr>
<tr><td>Share results with parents via conferences and weekly reports</td><td>Share results with parents via conferences, weekly reports, and report cards</td><td colspan="2">Share results with parents via conferences, passed fluency passages, and report cards</td><td>Share results with parents via conferences and report cards</td><td>Share results with parents via conferences, progress charts, and report cards</td></tr>
<tr><td>Use volunteers to listen to students read</td><td colspan="4">Use volunteers for “cold” and “hot” timings</td><td></td></tr>
</table>

The strategies we developed for computational fluency were at first schoolwide (Figure 5.3). That was until we saw our mid-year AIMSweb results; we had only bumped the schoolwide benchmark percentage from 22 percent to 33 percent. We knew we could do better so we crafted *grade*-level strategies (Figure 5.4) that were more specific. For example, our kindergarten teachers had not been sure how to support computational fluency when their students were still learning to identify numbers. The grade-level strategies helped by telling these teachers exactly what they could do, such as having kindergarteners practice composing (3 + 2 = 5) and decomposing (5 – 4 = 1) numbers to five. Creating grade-level strategies also invited creativity. In fourth grade, for example, the teachers developed a highly motivating incentive program. Their students earned attractive certificates and colorful wrist bands for memorizing math facts and demonstrating efficiency with standard algorithms. The kids responded with enthusiasm.

Figure 5.3. Math Strategies: Draft One

Theory of Action

If teachers provide uniformity in regards to instruction and student performance expectations, align computation curriculum with state standards, provide computational fluency practice, and use student performance data to drive instruction, ***then*** students' computational fluency will improve.

Schoolwide Strategies

- ☐ Teach efficient math computation procedures
- ☐ Schedule math fact practice
- ☐ Administer timed math fact tests
- ☐ Include motivational computation activities and provide multiple opportunities to practice computation skills
- ☐ Use computational fluency data to identify and remediate students with weak computation skills
- ☐ Involve students in setting computational fluency goals and charting their own progress
- ☐ Elicit parent support in regards to math fact practice

Figure 5.4. Math Strategies: Draft Two

Theory of Action

If teachers provide uniformity in regards to instruction and student performance expectations, align computation curriculum with state standards, provide computational fluency practice, and use student performance data to drive instruction, ***then*** students' computational fluency will improve.

Strategies

Kindergarten	1st Grade	2nd Grade	3rd Grade	4th Grade	5th Grade
Explicitly teach number sense, value, and symbols	Explicitly teach computation procedures and strategies	Explicitly teach computation procedures	Explicitly teach computation procedures; practice + and − with regrouping to mastery	Teach computation skills, math facts, and strengthen + & − facts	Explicitly teach efficient math computation procedures
Practice number formation and composing and decomposing numbers to 5	Practice math facts orally daily	Practice math facts daily		Practice math facts in small "chunks"	Schedule math fact practice daily
Elicit parent support re: number recognition	Administer math fact timed tests 3× week	Administer math fact timed tests		Administer math fact timed tests; include + & − assessments	Administer math fact timed tests

(Figure continues on next page.)

<table>
<tr><th>Kindergarten</th><th>1st Grade</th><th>2nd Grade</th><th>3rd Grade</th><th>4th Grade</th><th>5th Grade</th></tr>
<tr><td rowspan="2"></td><td colspan="3">Use fluency data to identify and assist at-risk students</td><td rowspan="2">Include students' "fluency & fact" status in parent progress notes; assign volunteers to work with low achievers</td><td rowspan="2">Use computational fluency data to identify and remediate at-risk students

Elicit parent support in regards to math practice</td></tr>
<tr><td>Elicit parent support with fact flash card practice</td><td>Elicit parent support with fact flash card practice & math games (put flash cards on supply list)</td><td>Elicit parent support with fact flash card practice (send cards home)</td></tr>
<tr><td></td><td></td><td colspan="2">Involve students in setting fluency goals and charting progress</td><td>Create incentives: Friday Club, assignment passes, art, certificates</td><td>Involve students in setting computational fluency goals and charting their own progress</td></tr>
<tr><td></td><td></td><td></td><td>Provide motivational computation activities & make real-world connections</td><td>Provide motivational computation activities; play Math Baseball; hold class competitions</td><td>Include motivational computation activities and provide multiple opportunities to practice computation skills</td></tr>
</table>

Preparing grade level strategies for computational fluency was a wise move. The grades 1 to 5 benchmark results rose from the midyear percentage of 33 to 47 percent, a +14 percent gain; the fall to spring gain was +25 percent. Not bad for an initiative with a start-to-finish implementation span of just 7 months. We have a long way to go of course, 47 percent is *far* too low. Nevertheless, the good news is that my teachers learned the power of preparing a Theory of Action, identifying strategies, and collecting evidence of progress. My teachers believe that they *can* raise student achievement. Will we raise computational fluency even further next year? We will keep tinkering until we do.

Craft Master Plans

Tony Fusek is a highly skilled carpenter, interior design expert, and home restoration genius. A few years back Tony purchased and restored a huge, multilevel home that was more than 120 years old. We're talking lath and plaster walls, peeling Victorian wallpaper, knob and tube wiring, claw footed bath tubs, and turn-of-the-century plumbing. The house had "good bones" but was otherwise a complete a wreck, so Tony chunked out the restoration work over a period of five years. He started by creating a master plan that outlined his restoration activities in sequence: electrical and plumbing replacement came first, for example, and refinishing the oak floors and repainting woodwork came last. When the work was finally complete, the home was stunning and the time and effort Tony put into the project was well worth it. Tony's master plan had successfully led him step by step through the long restoration process. "Just like anything," Tony said, "a good plan is the key—not just ideas in your head—a *written* plan with achievable short-term goals keeps you motivated and moving."

In the field of education master plans are equally valuable and I created one when my teachers and I determined that driving up math achievement would be our *raison d'être* for a few years. Our students weren't making gains on state tests and we needed to do something radically different. My first step was to research best practices in math instruction. I learned that to become successful math instructors, my teachers would need to accomplish the following (Nyland, 2008):

1. Understand what students should *know* and be able to *do*.
2. Know what to teach *prior* to the state assessment and what to teach *afterward* to prepare students for the next grade level.
3. Identify instructional materials that align to student performance expectations.

4. Convey content by using research supported instructional strategies, such as monitoring performance, correcting errors, and reteaching.
5. Collaborate with colleagues regarding effective instructional practices.
6. Use formative assessments during instruction and interim assessments every four to nine weeks to gauge mastery of concepts and skills.
7. Follow assessments with data meetings to discuss results, instructional implications, and further strategies.

These seven actions became the basis for a two-year effort that required extensive time, resources, and monitoring. For example, action one—understand what students should *know* and be able to *do*—was by itself an ambitious undertaking because our state had just issued updated math performance expectations that were considerably different from previous learning targets. To bring teachers up to speed with the performance expectations required ongoing training from math coaches, grade-level and faculty discussions about instructional practices, and time for teachers to adjust curriculum maps. Another obstacle to overcome was the lack of an aligned math program. Our current materials were out of sync at most grade levels and there were no funds to purchase a new one. Action 3—align instructional materials to performance expectations—would be difficult to achieve unless teachers had extra time to pull resources from supplemental textbooks, the state department of education website, and other sources. As it turned out, each of the seven actions listed in our Math Master Plan offered challenges, some unexpected. Action 5, which called for teacher collaboration for example, could not be fully implemented until we interrupted our math work to develop grade-level collaboration norms.

When you are confronting problems associated with the implementation of a master plan, it is vital to keep track of progress. Otherwise you won't know which teachers need support, who is ready to help others, and whether or not every action is being addressed. So teachers were surveyed regarding master plan implementation three times that first year. I used the simple rating scale that follows:

Implementation Rating Scale

0 = Not implemented

1 = Just Beginning to Implement

2 = Partially Implemented

3 = Fully Implemented

In January, I learned that teachers had made progress (Figure 5.5, page 118) compared to baseline data collected in October. Action 1 jumped from 1.35 to 3, for example, and action 6 from 1.96 to 2.4. At that time there were actions still requiring a lot of attention, however, such as collaborating with colleagues, using interim assessments, and holding data meetings to review and refine practices. We stayed on course through the end of the year and into the next. By the end of the second year every action had been implemented by every grade-level team.

Is your school moving forward with school improvement initiatives? If not, a simple, step-by-step master plan might be just what you need to get going.

Disaggregate Data

School improvement work requires up-to-the-minute data from reliable sources, but that's not all—unless data is perceived to be relevant by teachers, and used as a springboard for continued school improvement, then all the data in the universe won't get you anywhere. Here's a simple story that illustrates my point. For several years running, the percentage of spring parent conferences at my school was less than 80 percent. In an effort to raise the percentage, I increased communication with parents about the importance of meeting with their child's teacher, raised expectations—100 percent became the goal, and personally phoned parent "no shows." There was no significant change, however, until I took a bold move. I broke down the school's conference percentage teacher by teacher and openly shared the information with the faculty.

As Figure 5.6A (page 120) shows, the percentages ranged from a high of 100 percent to a low of 28 percent so the context within which the data was presented was crucial. Teachers with low results—nine had percentages that were 60 percent or less—were *not* blamed, chastised, or belittled. Instead, teachers with percentages *above* 80 percent were asked to share their successful scheduling techniques. I provided this opportunity at grade-level, curriculum, and faculty meetings. Over the next five years the school's conference percentage climbed steadily from a low of 78 percent to a high of 96 percent (Figure 5.6B, page 120).

(Text continues on page 121.)

Figure 5.5 Math Master Plan Status

MATH ACTION PLAN STATUS

Implementation Year: 1st

0 = Not Implemented	2 = Partially Implemented
1 = Just Beginning to Implement	3= Fully Implemented

Teachers understand what students should *know* and be able to *do*.

Ave. Implementation Score: October	January	Gain		Gr. K-1	Gr. 2	Gr. 3	Gr. 4	Gr. 5
1.35	3	1.65	October	0.5	1.5	2	1	1.75
			January	3	3	3	3	3

Teachers know what to teach *prior* to state assessments and what to teach *afterward* to prepare students for the next level.

Ave. Implementation Score: October	January	Gain		Gr. K-1	Gr. 2	Gr. 3	Gr. 4	Gr. 5
1.8	2.8	1	October	2	1	3	0	3
			January	2	3	3	3	3

Teachers have identified instructional materials that align to student performance expectations.

Ave. Implementation Score: October	January	Gain		Gr. K-1	Gr. 2	Gr. 3	Gr. 4	Gr. 5
2.44	2.2	-0.24	October	2	2.6	3	2	2.6
			January	3	1	3	1	3

Teachers convey content by using research supported instructional strategies, such as monitoring student performance, correcting errors, and reteaching.

Ave. Implementation Score: October	January	Gain		Gr. K-1	Gr. 2	Gr. 3	Gr. 4	Gr. 5
2.66	2.8	0.14	October	3	2.6	3	2	2.7
			January	3	3	3	2	3

Ave. Implementation Score			
October	January	Gain	
2.4	2.2	-0.2	**Teachers collaborate with colleagues regarding effective instructional practices.**

	Gr. K-1	Gr. 2	Gr. 3	Gr. 4	Gr. 5
October	2.5	0.5	3	3	3
January	3	2	3	0	3

October	January	Gain	
1.96	2.4	0.44	**Teachers use formative assessments during instruction.**

	Gr. K-1	Gr. 2	Gr. 3	Gr. 4	Gr. 5
October	1	1.8	3	2	2
January	1	3	3	2	3

October	January	Gain	
1.8	1.8	0	**Principals and teachers use interim assessments every 4 to 9 weeks to gauge student mastery of concepts and skills.**

	Gr. K-1	Gr. 2	Gr. 3	Gr. 4	Gr. 5
October	0	1.5	1	2	3
January	1	2	2	1	3

October	January	Gain	
1.35	1.6	0.25	**Follow assessments with data meetings to discuss results, instructional implications, and further strategies.**

	Gr. K-1	Gr. 2	Gr. 3	Gr. 4	Gr. 5
October	0	1.25	1	1.5	3
January	0	1	2	2	3

Figure 5.6 Parent–Teacher Conferences

A. Parent–Teacher Conference Percentages Year 1

Teacher	# Students	# Conferences Completed	Percentage
A	43	41	95
B	44	43	98
C	41	36	88
D	42	39	93
E	20	17	85
F	20	19	95
G	19	17	89
H	20	12	60
I	20	11	55
J	19	15	79
K	23	23	100
L	19	8	42
M	19	9	47
N	24	19	79
O	24	16	67
P	22	12	55
Q	23	20	87
R	24	12	50
S	24	22	92
T	18	5	28
U	24	24	100
V	22	12	55
W	20	18	90
X	22	12	55
Y	22	21	95
Total	**618**	**483**	**78**

B. Schoolwide Parent–Teacher Conference Percentages

78	Year One	93	Year Three	95	Year Five
83	Year Two	94	Year Four	96	Year Six

Why? Because once conference data was individualized, it became more meaningful. The results also became an impetus for action. As one teacher put it, "It was easy to be content with 80 percent until I saw other teachers doing way better." In fact, teachers throughout the school became interested in using new strategies, such as signing up parents for *spring* conferences during *fall* conferences, expanding evening conference opportunities, and having students share projects they are proud of—such as PowerPoint presentations—during conference meetings.

Individualizing data is an approach that will also breathe life into assessment results. Take oral reading fluency, math computation, reading comprehension, and state assessment scores and break them down. Compare teachers' student performance results to grade level, district, and state averages. This personalized information is even better when it includes entering and exit scores for every child as well as the class as a whole.

Mrs. Land's classroom results provide an example (Figure 5.7, page 122); note the sizable gains in reading (+23.6 percent) and math (+58 percent). These gains did not happen by chance. Mrs. Land has been tracking her student and classroom "entering" and "exit" scores for several years and continued to fine-tune instructional strategies to get the most from her time and from her students. Figure 5.8 (page 123) shows the math results for a cross-section of students from a recent class (a *shaded box* denotes the exit score).

To what does Mrs. Land owe her success? She gives credit to aligning lessons to state standards, teaching explicitly and intentionally, observing and immediately correcting student errors, and tracking individual student data over time.

Disaggregating schoolwide data heightens its meaning, improves data utility, and inspires corrective action. So the next time you get a chance to share data with teachers, be up close and personal—break it apart.

(Text continues on page 124.)

Figure 5.7 State Assessment Comparisons

5th GRADE READING			
Teacher	**Entering**	**Exiting**	**Growth**
A			
Mrs. Land	61	84.6	23.6
School A		**75.3**	
C			
D			
State		**73.9**	
E			
F			
G			
School B		**55.4**	
H			
I			
J			
K			

5th GRADE MATH			
Teacher	**Entering**	**Exiting**	**Growth**
A			
Mrs. Land	23	80.8	58
C			
School A		**61.9**	
State		**61.9**	
D			
E			
F			
School B		**52.7**	
G			
H			
I			
J			
K			

Figure 5.8 Student Entering and Exit Scores

Mathematics*

Student	4	3	2	1
	>427	400–427	375–399	<375
	Passing	Passing		
A		400		375
B		406	388	
C	429		397	
D	477	427		
E	445		397	
F		406		354
G	437		385	
H	464	410		
I		417	394	
J			380	367
K	437		391	
L		406		372
M		417		362
N	437	406		
O		428	388	
P			395	365
Q	454	417		
R		400		354
S		400	375	
T	429		383	
U		406	394	

* Shaded box denotes the exit score.

Suggested Readings

Copland, Michael A., & Knapp, Michael S. (2006). *Connecting leadership with learning: A framework for reflection, planning, and action*. Alexandria, VA: Association for Supervision and Curriculum Development.

McEwan, Elaine K. (2009). *10 Traits of highly effective schools: Raising the achievement bar for all students*. Thousand Oaks, CA: Corwin Press.

Power-up Staff Meetings

What are barriers to raising student achievement? Ask any educator and you will eventually hear that *time*—or rather the lack of—is one of the biggest obstacles. Makes sense—teachers need sufficient time to teach and students need sufficient time to learn. Likewise, time with teachers is *also* essential for school leaders striving to improve student performance. Principals and teachers need time *together* to compare their instructional approach, make sense of assessment data, create action plans, puzzle out the success—or failure—of interventions, and engage in professional development. To no one's surprise, improving schools requires time—lots of time—to substantially impact teaching and learning.

How do school leaders get this time? In many districts the school calendar is punctuated by "late starts," "early releases," and even full days off for staff and curriculum development. Sounds good at first glance, but unfortunately, the focus of this "extra time" is usually predetermined by district-level committees, grant-funded programs, or the teacher contract—time for teacher collaboration, for example, has become an expectation. In my district, considerable professional development time is also lost to health-and-safety training, fund-raising endeavors, insurance presentations, and district and board policy reviews.

Of course meeting *after* hours for school improvement work is an option, but many teachers can't participate because of family obligations or extracurricular events. There are also teachers who *won't* participate unless they are paid for time that falls outside normal work hours. This expectation is fair, but, unfortunately, funds for extended hours are hard to come by.

Some school leaders look to "release time" *during* the school day as the best approach but this requires money for substitute teachers and enough substitute teachers to go around. Another downside is that release time does not free the *entire* faculty to work together.

Given the aforementioned disadvantages, I learned the value of setting staff meetings aside for school improvement work. I meet thirty minutes a week, nearly every week of the school year, with my certificated staff of thirty teachers and specialists. We get together in the morning, before school, to avoid conflicts with after-school meetings, coaching obligations, and extracurricular activities. Thirty minutes may not sound like a lot of time, especially with a large faculty, but I have learned a few tricks. Here are the best:

- Create meeting norms and review and evaluate adherence regularly. Expectations should include arriving on time, listening attentively, avoiding side conversations, and sharing information in a time conscious manner.
- Plan staff meetings a year in advance and have a specific outcome in mind for each session (Figure 5.9). The outcomes might be a list of suggestions for improving students' study habits, norms for grade level meetings, the completion of program evaluation surveys, or an analysis of mid-year math scores. Always go into a meeting knowing *exactly* what you want to achieve.

Figure 5.9. Staff Meeting Plan

Month	Date	Topic
September	♦ 2: District In-service ♦ 3: Staff Meeting ♦ 15: Staff Meeting ♦ 22: Late Start Meeting ♦ 29: Staff Meeting	District Workshop Options State Assessment Review; Staff Norms; Center Meeting Team Collaboration Norms First Aid Training Teachers and the Law Review
October	♦ 6: Staff Meeting ♦ 13: Staff Meeting ♦ 20: Late Start Meeting ♦ 27: Staff Meeting	Computational Fluency Training Computational Fluency Cycle of Inquiry Oral Fluency Training Oral Fluency Cycle of Inquiry
November	♦ 3: Late Start Meeting ♦ 10: Staff Meeting ♦ 17: Staff Meeting ♦ 24: No Meeting	Reading Program Review Reading Program Review School Improvement Plan (Parent–Teacher Conferences)

(Figure continues on next page.)

Month	Date	Topic
December	♦ 1: Late Start Meeting ♦ 8: Staff Meeting ♦ 15: Staff Meeting ♦ 22: No Meeting ♦ 29: No Meeting	State Assessment Review Instructional Frameworks Review Instructional Frameworks Review (Winter Break) (Winter Break)
January	♦ 5: Staff Meeting ♦ 12: Late Start Meeting ♦ 19: Staff Meeting ♦ 26: Staff Meeting	Computational Fluency Mid-Year Data Writing Best Practices Oral Reading Fluency Mid-Year Data STAR Reading and Accelerated Reader Data
February	♦ 2: Late Start Meeting ♦ 9: Staff Meeting ♦ 16: Staff Meeting ♦ 23: Staff Meeting	Writing Best Practices Classroom Based Assessments Classroom Based Assessments Student Engagement
March	♦ 2: Staff Meeting ♦ 9: Staff Meeting ♦ 16: Staff Meeting ♦ 23: Late Start Meeting ♦ 30: No Meeting	Student Goal Setting Student Progress Monitoring Formative Assessments Formative Assessments (Parent-Teacher Conferences)
April	♦ 6: No Meeting ♦ 13: Staff Meeting ♦ 20: Late Start Meeting ♦ 27: Staff Meeting	(Spring Break) Science Overview Science Overview State Testing Proctor Training
May	♦ 4: Late Start Meeting ♦ 11: No Meeting ♦ 18: No Meeting ♦ 25: No Meeting	End of Year Academic Focus (State Testing) (State Testing) (State Testing)
June	♦ 1: Staff Meeting ♦ 8: Late Start Meeting ♦ 15: Staff Meeting	Achievement Data Review Achievement Data Review School Goal Review

- Align meeting agendas to school improvement work—use action plans, Theories of Action, and supporting strategies as guides. Don't forget to cover adopted instructional programs—alignment with state standards, assessment options, and remediation materials.

- Stay with a topic for as long as it takes to reach your intended outcome. If you want to develop questions and rubrics for teacher interviews, for example, it might take two or three faculty meetings in succession to get the job done.

- Be a good teacher—start every meeting by announcing the purpose and expected outcomes. Use a good "anticipatory set" as well. If you are passing out test results, for example, don't just say: "Here are the spring state assessment scores." Jazz things up by inviting teacher teams to find "data trends" and offering a reward, such as "leave school early" passes to the group that finds the most.

- Review the previous meeting's accomplishments, especially when you are running a series of meetings on the same topic. Be visual—hold up the charts, lists, posters, or surveys that were completed at the last meeting and remind teachers of their significance. Teachers' participation improves when they see that they are getting somewhere.

- Use organizational tools. When my teachers arrive for meetings in our school library, for example, they find "popup" cards on tables announcing table groups, such as Grade 1, special education, or intermediate versus primary. There are also detailed agendas set out along with needed handouts at each chair. The agendas outline the purpose of the meeting, the activities, and the expected outcomes.

- Control time by creating agendas with time lines and using a signal, like a bell, to gain and maintain teacher attention. Protocols, which provide procedures for accomplishing a task, also save time. Examples are available from such online sources as the National School Reform Faculty (www.nsrfharmony.org) and Visible Thinking (www.pz.harvard.edu).

- Identify facilitators to lead group work. You might want to appoint and orient these folks ahead of time if the meeting tasks are complex. I pull facilitators from my Principal Advisory Council because its membership includes teachers who are already perceived as leaders. If the meeting work is pretty straight forward, however, instructions are outlined on the agenda. Directions usually include the selection of group facilitators (the staff member with the largest pet) and recorder/reporters (the owner of the newest car).

- Boost meeting engagement by creating activities that get your teachers highly involved. Staff members enjoy talking about their work; creating products such as posters, charts, and recommendation lists; critiquing actions plans (Figure 5.10, page 129), mission statements, and discipline guides; producing skits to illustrate a concept or teach a skill; reviewing articles and book excerpts; completing surveys (Figure 5.11, page 130); and field testing teaching tools, such as scoring guides (Figure 5.12, page 131). When you think "staff meeting" you should think "workshop."

Finding time to work together with teachers is a challenge for most school leaders but artfully organized staff meetings will realize plenty of opportunities. So if you are pressed for school improvement time, make *your* staff meetings prime time.

(Text continues on page 132.)

Figure 5.10. Staff Meeting: School Improvement Plan

OVERVIEW (5 minutes)

Focus:	School Improvement Plan – 2nd Draft
Purpose:	Critique student achievement goals
Outcome:	Contribute ideas for the final draft of the School Improvement Plan

Groups:	Grade Level and Departmental
Facilitator:	The person with the *largest* pet.
Recorder:	The person with the *smallest* pet.

GROUP TASK (15 minutes):

There are five (5) proposed student achievement goals. These goals align with the School District Strategic Plan and our previous School Improvement Plan.

Read each goal and discuss whether or not this goal—if implemented—would help us move forward.

- ☐ **Circle** the goals you think we should pursue. Feel free to make revisions.
- ☐ Put an **X** through the goals we should delete.
- ☐ **Jot down** any additional goals you would like us to focus on.

GROUP REPORTS (10 minutes)

Each group's recorder will get a chance to summarize outcomes.

Return group notes to the Principal.

Figure 5.11. Staff Meeting: Math Assessments

OVERVIEW (5 minutes)

Focus: Math Assessments

Purpose: Collect ideas for a grade level math assessment

Outcome: Survey responses will be collected and summarized for further discussions

Groups: Grade Level Teams (Specialists: Join a team of your choice)

Facilitator: The person who travels the furthest to school

Recorder: The person who lives the closest to school

GROUP TASK (25 minutes):

Question 1: What day to day math assessments are you using?

- Written assignments?
- Questioning?
- Unit tests?
- Computational fluency progress monitoring?
- Observing math tasks or activities?
- State assessment practice tests?
- Other?

Question 2: What evidence of learning do you collect?

- Corrected assignments?
- Portfolio collections?
- Performance ratings?
- Rubric evaluations?
- Informal Notes?
- Other?

Question 3: How could a common Grade-Level Math Assessment help you?

- How would it be used?
- How often should it be given?
- Who should correct the assessment?
- What types of problems should be included?

__	Computation problems	__	Multiple choice
__	Short answer	__	Story problems
__	Math tasks	__	True/false

- Other?

Return Your Answers to the Principal

Figure 5.12. Staff Meeting: Writing Evaluation

Writers on Writing

No passion in the world is equal to the passion to alter someone else's draft.

H.G. Wells (1866–1946)

Your manuscript is both good and original; but the part that is good is not original, and the part that is original is not good.

Samuel Johnson (1709–1784)

OVERVIEW (5 minutes)

Focus: Writing Evaluation

Purpose: Field-test the new writing scoring guides developed at previous meetings

Outcome: Suggestions for improving the scoring guides

Groups: Grade-Level Teams (Specialists: Join a team of your choice)

Facilitator: The person who cooked the biggest turkey on Thanksgiving

Recorder: The person who cooked the smallest Thanksgiving bird

INDIVIDUAL TASK (10 minutes)

Using your grade level's new Writing Scoring Guide, assess the two letters written to the principal by students from your grade level.

____

____

____

GROUP DISCUSSION (10 minutes)

Did the new scoring guide help you determine the quality of the students' writing?

____

____

____

What suggestions do you have for improving the guide? Return notes to the principal.

____

____

____

Engineer Sustainability

What's my biggest problem? I can answer that question in just two words—staff turnover. I arrived at my school eight years ago and have seen thirty-four dynamite teachers come and go. In the upcoming school year, only *six* of twenty classroom teaching positions will be filled by teachers who have been with me throughout the duration of my principalship. Why the loss of so many teachers? The reasons include the reconfiguration of our school district's elementary schools five years ago—I lost 50 percent of my teachers; budget shortfalls that precipitated staff reductions; child care leaves; voluntary transfers to the secondary level; and the unfortunate fact that many school districts in our region pay teachers more. It was high teacher turnover that precipitated my keen interest in "sustainability," which Fullan defines as "the capacity of a system to engage in the complexities of continuous improvement consistent with deep values of human purpose" (2005, p. ix). Unfortunately, when the players keep shifting, sustaining purposeful work is daunting.

Sustainability is also difficult when faculties are stable. Systematic, schoolwide approaches to raising student achievement are hard to get going and once implemented, even harder to maintain. It can take multiple years to identify goals, craft action plans, build staff capacity to carry out the mission, and realize results. Some teachers may reject the mission at the onset; others may get on board initially but then be resistant to learning new skills. There are also teachers looking for a quick fix who lose their enthusiasm when obstacles appear insurmountable.

Is achieving sustainability hopeless? Not at all—my school made AYP (Adequate Yearly Progress) in 2010 in every applicable category, including special education and low income. This hard-won designation was the result of a systemwide approach to boosting student achievement, a laser like focus on our mission, unflagging persistence, and the following strategies:

- *Set Expectations:* Your school's norms ought to include professional expectations, such as supporting every student's learning, staying current with educational research, implementing *best practices*, and engaging in professional development activities.

- *Clarify the Mission:* You should begin each school year by reviewing your school improvement vision and goals. This includes revisiting previous action plans, Theories of Actions, intervention strategies, and supporting data. New staff members also need to hear *why* the mission was chosen in the first place. Be sure to share the history, such as student achievement setbacks or major obstacles; the educational research; and the thinking behind your objectives.

- *Identify Core Beliefs:* Do you believe you have a moral obligation to improve *every* student's learning (Fullan, 2005)? Do you believe that schools are more effective when teachers align instruction or that achievement data should drive program decisions? Then reiterate core beliefs with your teachers. Use inspiring stories, powerful professional articles, and illustrative videos to get your ideas across.
- *Update Plans:* Pull out the previous year's work—action plans, Theory of Actions, strategies—and update them. This is a good way to review plans with teachers, discuss the validity of previous interventions, and elicit suggestions from new staff members. Veteran staff that have benefited from professional readings and training over the summer may also see areas that need tweaking.
- *Maintain Capacity:* What does your staff need to know and be able to do to carry out your mission? This probably includes knowing state curricular standards and assessment requirements; how to effectively use adopted instructional programs; administer, score, and record schoolwide assessments; and work collaboratively with other teachers. Regularly review key concepts and skills with the entire faculty and provide in-depth training for the newbies.
- *Use Teacher Leaders:* Your teachers have more credibility than you do. They are in the trenches every day and know the ins and outs of grade-level standards, curriculum, instructional practices, and assessment. Use these experts to teach new staff and conduct reviews for the rest of the faculty.
- *Study Trend Data:* Periodically review student achievement trends with teachers. Is there steady growth in reading? Has science progress stagnated? Are second language learners behind the general population in writing? Looking at school, district, and state level achievement results and data trends will verify the efficacy of your school's improvement plans and serve as the impetus for change. Don't forget to make data meaningful to teachers by breaking apart schoolwide results by grade level, classroom, and student.
- *Track Individual Student Progress:* Improving student performance won't overwhelm teachers if they view it as happen-

ing one kid at a time. So involve teachers is tracking student progress. In particular, pay attention to students who are at the bottom of the class academically or who have failed past state assessments. These students are *not* hopeless. Most have improved significantly over time, so always project that *every* student is deserving and capable of growth.

- *Be a Cheerleader:* School Improvement efforts often involve change, such as implementing new textbook adoptions, academic screenings, instructional frameworks, and student progress monitoring systems. Take time to applaud your teachers' hard work.
- *Celebrate Successes:* Never miss an opportunity to celebrate success. When you see growth anywhere in the system, get the word out. The good feeling that emanates from good news is unfailingly uplifting.

How do you sustain school improvement endeavors? Fullan tells us that it is "the actions embedded in the norms, competencies, and practices of the organization" that "move the organization forward" (2008, p. 126). So whether your staff is stable or in a constant state of flux, maintain school improvement momentum through proactive leadership.

Suggested Reading

Smith, Lew. (2008). *Schools that change: Evidence-based improvement and effective change leadership*. Thousand Oaks, CA: Corwin Press.

Summing Up

- No matter the makeup of the school, the achievement challenges there, or the school's barriers to success, improving student achievement is the primary job of school leaders.
- Strengthening student performance requires *every* staff member's participation.
- A solid Theory of Action delineates the *cause* and *effect* relationship between educators' actions and outcomes.
- Data that is broken down by student, classroom, and grade level has more meaning.
- Create multiyear master plans for improving teaching and learning.

- Take advantage of staff meeting time for school improvement work.
- Sustain school improvement efforts by setting expectations, reviewing improvement plans, maintaining capacity, and celebrating accomplishments.

Making Connections

- What are the barriers to student success in your school district? How are they being addressed? Are you collecting data to track progress? What refinements do you need to make?
- Is there alignment among the teachers and specialists at your school? Could staff members reach agreement about the school's mission, improvement plan, and instructional practices? If not, how could you make this happen?

Strengthening Professional Practice

- Write a Theory of Action for a subject area in your school that needs to be strengthened. Prepare an "if–then" statement that shows the linkage between actions and outcomes. Add schoolwide or grade-level strategies.
- What steps are you taking to sustain efforts to raise student achievement? Make a list of steps that you would like to add and include a timeline for implementation.

Theme 6

Derailing Leadership Distress

> *...[I]f you do not take care of yourself regularly, you will eventually have nothing left to give. You will...have no energy to care for others, to do good work, or to make a difference in the world.*
>
> — Dr. Paul Foxman, (2007, p. 98)

My mind was racing as I left a school board meeting that had finally drawn to a close after running into overtime. Although I was tired after a long, hectic work day, I felt energized by the meeting's focus—raising student achievement in mathematics. Elementary and secondary principals had reported the innovative ways they were helping students make gains and I had picked up strategies I was eager to try. As I was about to enter my car, an exhausted-looking colleague approached to air his concern about the school board's increasing emphasis on raising student achievement. "I'm not sure I can do much more," he lamented before unexpectedly asking, "What motivates you anyway?" I wish I could say I had shared an inspirational core belief or a lofty mission statement, but in truth, my first response was: "Fear." I thought at the time I was making a joke and so did my colleague—we both laughed then headed for home. But as I drove the familiar roads back to my family I realized how true my reply *had* been—I feared that I would be unable to improve every child's learning, to keep up with job demands, to maintain a high level of performance, and to support the people I served. What I didn't know was that *fear* is a manifestation of *anxiety*, which, in turn, is triggered by *stress* (Foxman, 2007).

How stressful is the principal's job? In *Leadership Teaming: The Superintendent–Principal Relationship*, I expressed heartfelt enthusiasm for the school leadership role, while taking note of the stress producers: inadequate funding, unrealistic workloads, incompetent teachers, dangerous students, emotionally unstable parents, and contentious unions to name just a few (West & Derrington, 2009). How bad is stress? Ginsberg (2008) cautions us that when stress is unmanaged it may lead to serious health, social, and emotional problems.

The good news is that stress *is* manageable. Theme 6 provides a wide range of tips to help school leaders identify stress sources and symptoms; initiate stress prevention activities; set realistic goals; manage resources and time; and strengthen leadership capacity. School leaders who derail leadership distress will stay on top of demands, make a difference in their schools, and enjoy the benefits of long, rewarding careers.

Craft Stress Response Plans

I was once diagnosed with a "pinched nerve" in my upper back that I attributed to my competitive—and admittedly irrational—efforts to do more chin ups than any of my fifth graders. However, one of my doctors, after inventorying my principal responsibilities, insisted the painful flareup was caused by *stress*. I was a seasoned administrator, so this diagnosis surprised me: Wasn't I immune to the tensions of leadership life? That's not to suggest that the stressful events principals experience aren't significant—there are defiant students who kick chairs across classrooms, angry parents who hurl insults at undeserving staff members, and insubordinate teachers who inexplicably defy principals' directives. Other less dramatic stressors—but no less powerful in regards to impact—are orchestrating efforts to raise student achievement; managing tight school budgets; taking employee disciplinary action; and making difficult decisions, such as whether or not to cut a popular but underperforming program.

Given that stress is inevitable, how can one tell when *routine* stress has become *too* much stress? Dr. Paul Foxman, the impressive author of *Dancing with Fear: Controlling Stress and Creating a Life Beyond Panic and Anxiety*, informs us that "headaches, backaches, difficulty relaxing, muscle twitches, and low energy" may signal an overabundance of stress (2007, p. 62). You can add to Foxman's list of stress indicators a compromised immune system, irritability, insomnia, and depression (Queen & Queen, 2005).

Sound scary? Put your fears to rest. You can effectively manage stress by recognizing the signs of overload, identifying stress producers, and crafting response plans that keep stress generators under control.

I can tell when I am overstressed—I wake up in the dead of night fretting about work. About the time of the "pinched nerve" episode, which materialized in late April, my late night worries included the following:

Responsibilities	Major Stressors
School	In May, my teachers and I prepare class lists for the following school year. Sadly, however, six low seniority teachers will lose their jobs as a consequence of budget cuts. Their positions will be filled by veteran teachers from other schools but we won't know *who* these teachers will be until the end of June. To complicate matters, once the low seniority teachers get RIF notices, other teachers in the district might apply for reassignment to the newly vacated positions. I project that more than one-third of our teacher assignments could change. Final evaluations for thirty certificated staff members are coming due but I still have several required observations to complete. I also need to make a few more "drop-in" classroom visits. We've just enrolled a first grader who appears to have a behavior disorder—her discipline record from the previous school is nine pages long. The teacher assigned to this tyke is in a panic because the child has been defiant toward adults and physically aggressive with classmates.
Professional Activities	An education journal needs a book review soon—I've read the book and made a few notes but can't find time to work on the review. I need to prepare a presentation for a regional curriculum directors' meeting but other commitments keep interfering.

To reduce stressful feelings, gain control of my responsibilities, and stop worrying, I craft "stress-response plans." I pare down expectations, revise timelines, or delegate tasks to someone else. Note the examples that follow, which include response plan strategies.

Responsibilities	Major Stressors
School	In May, my teachers and I prepare class lists for the following school year. Sadly, however, six low seniority teachers will lose their jobs as a consequence of budget cuts. Their positions will be filled by veteran teachers from other schools but we won't know *who* these teachers will be until the end of June. To complicate matters, once the low seniority teachers get RIF notices, other teachers in the district might apply for reassignment to the newly vacated positions. I project that more than one-third of our teacher assignments could change. **Response Plan:** Create the class lists in August, inviting teacher volunteers to participate. In preparation, require teachers to complete a "placement card" for each student that includes instructional, behavioral, and special services information, as well as recommendations for teachers by name or style. Final evaluations for thirty teachers are coming due but I still have several required observations to complete. I also need to make a few more "drop-in" classroom visits. **Response Plan:** Spend the remainder of the week completing observations and catching up on class visits. Start the final evaluations in May (write two per day at home prior to the start of the school day). We've just enrolled a first grader who appears to have a behavior disorder—her discipline record from the previous school is nine pages long. The teacher assigned to this tyke is in a panic because the child has been defiant toward adults and physically aggressive with classmates. **Response Plan:** Tomorrow schedule a meeting with the Student Services Team to review the child's record and develop a management plan. This plan may include starting the student part-time and alternative placement in the behavior room for a portion of the day.

Professional Activities	An education journal needs a book review soon—I've read the book and made a few notes but can't find time to work on the review. **Response Plan:** Find a colleague to do the review. I need to prepare a presentation for a regional curriculum directors' meeting but other commitments keep interfering. **Response Plan:** Ask another principal to copresent and set a date to plan the presentation together.

How do you know a response plan is solid? It should immediately reduce anxiety feelings. So the next time you lay awake fretting about work obligations, start crafting stress-response plans.

Suggested Reading

Foxman, Paul. (2007). *Dancing with fear: Controlling stress and creating a life beyond panic and anxiety*. Second edition. Alameda, CA: Hunter House.

Stay Healthy

When I was a college student I was lucky to land summer jobs as a housekeeper and waitress at hotels around Lake Tahoe, a beautiful resort area in the mountains of northern California. I had no car at the time so I used a bike to get to work, shop at local stores, and—in my off time—visit lakeside beaches. I worked hard but the physical demands of waiting tables, cleaning hotel rooms, and peddling my bike kept me in great shape. As an added bonus, my jobs ended in the early afternoon so there was plenty of time for rest and relaxation. Staying physically fit and emotionally healthy was a breeze.

For the busy school leader "staying healthy" may seem impossible. Work responsibilities are all-consuming and it is not unusual for principals to work a ten- to twelve-hour day without a break. There are also night events that cut into precious time, making high-fat, salt-laden "fast food" the default meal on the run. Given the time crunch, how do school leaders fit in exercise, nutritious eating, and restorative rest breaks?

Good health begins with a commitment to healthy lifestyle practices. Depending upon personal health challenges, this might include a trip to the doctor for a comprehensive checkup, joining a gym, consulting a counselor, or enrolling in a weight-loss clinic. For optimum impact, however, don't stop there. Incorporate healthy practices into your day-to-day work life. Here are some easy-to-implement strategies:

Strategy	Examples
Pair a healthy activity with a work-related task.	Need more supervision at a challenging recess? Referee football or soccer. You will reduce behavior problems and get some valuable exercise. Combine a brisk walk in and around your school with other jobs, such as checking on bus arrivals, making personal contacts, and delivering "good news" notes. Got a student ready to blow? Offer to take the youngster on a stroll. You will *both* benefit from the excursion.
Take control of your food intake.	Keep healthy foods, such as dried fruit, raw nuts, and low-salt crackers, in your office. If you have your own snack stash, it will be easier to pass up the pastries that are a standard feature of most staff rooms. Bring a nutritious lunch *every* day. Yogurt and a granola bar or a cup of soup and crackers, for example, are quick, cheap, and easy. Graciously accept the calorie-laden treats that staff, clients, and students bestow upon you, then covertly deep-six the stuff once your benefactors are out of sight.
Get moving!	Help supervise your most demanding lunch period—the one with the highest discipline referrals. You will get to know your students, keep behavior under control, and get great exercise from pacing up and down the cafeteria tables. Keep sneakers handy so that you can participate in a PE class—you'll get the blood flowing and the teacher and students will welcome your participation. When there is freight to move, cardboard to haul to recycling bins, or litter to be picked up, help out. You will score points with your custodial staff and get a valuable break from sedentary desk work.

Strategy	Examples
Relax.	Do your shoulder and neck muscles tense up? Check out the ergonomics of your workstation. Is the chair too low, the keyboard too high, or the monitor sitting off center? Correcting these problems will go a long way toward relaxing tight muscle fibers. Visit a kindergarten and help a tyke with a challenging task, such as cutting and gluing. You'll get a huge smile in return—a guaranteed blood-pressure reducer. Feeling frazzled? Drop into the library when your librarian is reading a storybook to children. The kids will love seeing you join their circle and you will get a few moments to relax.

Incorporating healthy practices isn't rocket science, but it *does* require a strong commitment and thoughtful planning. Better health and career longevity, however, makes these efforts well worth it. Get started today.

Suggested Reading

Queen, J. Allen, & Queen, Patsy S. (2005). *The frazzled principal's wellness plan: Reclaiming time, managing stress, and creating a healthy lifestyle.* Thousand Oaks, CA: Corwin Press.

Set Realistic Goals

School goal setting is a vital leadership responsibility. Without well-developed goals, principals and teachers may not fulfill their school's mission and carryout priority responsibilities. Goal setting may sound easy for administrators who believe it to be just another "to-do" list, but in fact, identifying the "right" goals can be tricky. Early in my career I made several mistakes. First, I relied upon teacher input as my primary source for school-improvement goals. This input was gathered via comprehensive surveys that spanned every aspect of school life—from teaching and learning to facility upgrades; from parent involvement to health and safety. Hundreds of goals were generated by enthusiastic faculty members, making determining priorities near to impossible. Second, I naively believed that *writing* a goal equated with *accomplishing* the goal. So my teachers and I optimistically developed a boat load of goals that we had no hope in reaching given time constraints and competing demands. And, finally, some of our goals were out of sync with the work we had done the previous year, current student achievement data, and the latest school district initiative. The overabundance of misaligned goals was well intentioned, but didn't make sense. This inept approach to goal setting brought unnecessary frustration—which was stress we could do without.

I am smarter now; when it is time to set goals I use *four* sources of information:

- School District Strategic Plan
- School Goal Plan from the Preceding Year
- Student Achievement Data
- Faculty Members

I chose the first three sources—the strategic plan (Granite Falls School District, 2010), previous school goals, and achievement data—with alignment in mind. Figure 6.1 shows how easily goals can be integrated with other initiatives, such as my district's strategic plan and a school leadership project being done under the auspices of the Washington State Leadership Academy.

Despite drawing from multiple sources, I didn't end up with an overabundance of goals. I gained control by drafting the goals myself after careful consideration of previous school improvement work, the most current achievement data, and school district expectations. The goals were then presented to my advisory council whose members were invited to critique and fine-tune them. After making needed revisions—deleting or adding goals, revising others—the goals went to the entire faculty for approval. Because the goals incorporated previous work and aligned with district initiatives, faculty approval was easy to come by. As a final step, I aligned my own professional goals to our newly adopted school goals (Figure 6.2, page 147).

Arland astutely observes that "when an archer misses the mark, he turns and looks for the fault within himself" (*Get Smart*, 2004, p. 86). When it comes to goal setting, the fault might be that the school leader has identified *too* many goals or goals that are out of sync with current reality. This leads to unnecessary frustration on the part of the leader and the faculty. So avoid goal-setting aggravations—set relevant, realistic goals.

(Text continues on page 149.)

Figure 6.1. Goal Plan Integration Guide

	Granite Falls School District Strategic Plan	Granite Falls School District Math Action Plan	Mountain Way Elementary School Improvement Plan
Mission	Prepare students to achieve their greatest potential.	Provide a system that supports teachers and staff in aligning K-12 math curriculum, research-based instruction, and assessments so that each child will meet or exceed math performance standards?	We will provide children with a stimulating academic program, a safe and supportive learning environment, and the knowledge and skills needed to become successful family members, productive adults, and contributing citizens.
Theory of Action	Effective systems have a shared understanding of powerful instruction. Effective districts have coherence across the system. Effective districts work from data and act strategically.	Effective systems have a shared understanding of powerful instruction. Effective systems have coherence across the system. Effective districts work from data and act strategically.	**Goal:** Learn about and then *apply* the "theory of action" concept in regards to students' math computation and oral reading fluency. **Goal:** Field-test the district's newly developed instructional frameworks for teachers.

(Figure continues on next page.)

	Granite Falls School District Strategic Plan	Granite Falls School District Math Action Plan	Mountain Way Elementary School Improvement Plan
Target 1	Improve the instructional core: the connection between teachers' knowledge and skill, students' engagement in their own learning, and academically challenging content.	Develop shared understanding of essential components of highly effective math instruction. Align math curriculum with performance standards. Develop formative and summative assessments.	**Goal:** Implement Year Two of Mountain Way's Math Action Plan. **Goal:** Use data from academic screenings, in the moment assessments, and interim testing to guide instruction.
Target 2	Sustain and build on our collaborative culture among students, parents, community, and staff.		**Goal:** Develop and follow norms for staff collaboration. **Goal:** Look for ways to increase collaboration time.
Target 3	Support the instructional core by maintaining and providing the necessary structures and systems.		**Goal:** Review services to students with behavior challenges and determine how needs can be met given the available staff.

Figure 6.2. Principal Goals

2009–10 PRINCIPAL GOAL STATUS REPORT
Mountain Way Elementary

LEADERSHIP

Major Responsibilities

- School Operation & Management
  See attachment
- Mathematics School Improvement Plan
  Year Two Plan: In progress
- Theory of Action & Instructional Strategies Projects
  Computational Fluency: Completed
  Oral Reading Fluency: In progress
- Staff Collaboration Norms
  Collaboration In-services: 2 Completed
  Department and Grade-Level Norms: Completed
  Observation of Implementation: 1 Cycle Completed
- Instructional Frameworks Introduction
  Principal Advisory Council Introduction: 2 Completed
  Faculty In-services: 2 Completed

Committees

- Washington State Leadership Academy Team
- Instructional Core Assessment Committee
  Assessment Practices Presentations: 3 Completed
- Principal Advisory Council (Coordinator)
- Schoolwide Intervention Team
- Special Education Student Services Team
- Highly Capable Student Selection Committee
- Time for Kids Fundraiser Committee (Coordinator)

Professional Development Leader

- Book Studies Leader
  Dancing with Fear (2007, Hunter House) by Dr. Paul Foxman
  Setting Limits in the Classroom (2003, Three Rivers Press) by Robert J. MacKenzie
- Professional Development for Teachers—Weekly Staff Meetings
  Data Analysis
  First Aid
  Code of Ethics and Collaboration
  Student Guidance and Discipline

(Figure continues on next page.)

Strategic Plan
Computational Fluency
Math Standards Update
School Improvement Plan
Oral Reading Fluency
Reading Assessment Update
Assessment Proctoring (Scheduled for April)

- Late-Start Professional Development Sessions (Coordinator/Presenter)
  Skyword Database Use
  Team Collaboration
  Math Assessment Update
  Instructional Frameworks
  Writing Style (scheduled for April)

PROFESSIONAL PREPARATION & SCHOLARSHIP

- Washington State Leadership Academy Trainings, Coaching Opportunities
- Regional Curriculum Meetings: 1 (scheduled for 2nd meeting in May)
- Washington State Kappan Editorial Board
- Professional Readings
  Phi Delta Kappan
  NAESP *Principal*
  ASCD *Educational Leadership*
  Dancing with Fear: Dr. Paul Foxman
  Setting Limits in the Classroom: Robert J. MacKenzie
  Social Intelligence: Daniel Goleman
  Teaching Grammar: Amy Benjamin & Joan Berger
  What Do You Say When?: Hal Holloman & Peggy Yates
  4 Core Factors for School Success: Todd Whitaker & Jeffrey Zoul
- Professional Writing
  Article for *Principal* magazine (selected for publishing)
  Book for Eye On Education (in progress)

EFFORT TOWARD IMPROVEMENT

- WSLA Coach: Teacher Conference Feedback
- Washington State Consultant: Collaboration project
- Principal Evaluation Form for Certificated Staff

INTEREST IN PUPILS, EMPLOYEES, PATRONS, & SUBJECTS

Students

- Visited classrooms and assisted students

- Supervised 5th grade lunch, which created student contact opportunities
- Implemented the weekly K-3 Talented Tigers and grades 4–5 Lunch Bunch Program
- Coordinated the grades 4 and 5 Awards Assemblies
- Organized the grade 5 Graduation Program

Staff

- Fine-tuned the staff *Code of Ethics and Collaboration*
- Participated in Learning Walks

Parent & Community

- Provided school and district updates at monthly PIK meetings
- Communicated via *Tiger Tales Newsletters* and monthly bulletins
- Participated in the School Volunteer Luncheon
- Acted as the school's liaison with community agencies
- Involved parents via Literacy Nights, Concerts, Open House, Parent–Teacher Conferences, field trips, parent meetings, Washington Reading Corp volunteering

EVALUATION OF STAFF

- Scheduled fall, winter, and spring progress conferences with certificated staff
- Observed and provided feedback to affirm instructional skill
- Covered classes so that teachers could observe colleagues

Stay on Top of Your Workload

I love sardonic quips—especially ones that capture the complexities of the workplace. Such is the case with the following bon mot: "Chaos is not just a theory—it's my life." This witticism graced a thank you card from a newbie principal I had helped through several tough situations. I understood the sentiment—chaos is a salient feature of leadership life. If things get *too* chaotic, however, even the best administrator can become overwhelmed and discouraged. This may have been the case with the retiring principal I replaced who left behind a lapel pin that read: "Since I gave up hope I feel much better." Although this wry pronouncement was meant to be humorous there is an uncomfortable edge to it. Had this veteran school leader *really* found his job hopeless? I keep the pin as a reminder to stay on top of my job.

There are several ways I maintain control of my workload—by setting goals, charting my responsibilities, and using a daily checklist.

- *Goals:* My school and professional goal plans (see Figures 6.1, page 145, and 6.2, page 147) keep me focused on major objectives. I check these plans weekly and as I do so ask: "Am I moving forward?" If not, it's time to "chunk" objectives into doable tasks and create a completion timeline.

- ♦ *Checklist:* I use a daily checklist (Figure 6.3) to guide my actions throughout the busy school day. When I arrive at work the daily checklist is the first thing I grab; it reminds me to:
  - Attend morning meetings, such as student services, staff, and intervention team.
  - Check my calendar, tickler file, and e-mail for scheduled meetings and events.
  - Touch base with my secretary and part-time assistant.
  - Check voicemail, e-mail, and snail mail.
  - Visit classrooms or complete scheduled teacher observations.
  - Handle discipline referrals, including contact with parents.
  - Return phone calls.
  - Prepare documents for copying.
  - Complete reports or projects that are coming due.
  - Plan my day by setting goals, selecting priority projects, and noting scheduled meetings and events. All of which are jotted down in shorthand at the bottom of the checklist.
- ♦ *Responsibilities:* Another organizer that has proven to be invaluable is a chart that identifies my major assignments and those of my part-time Teacher on Special Assignment (Figure 6.4, page 152). I can easily scan the chart to remind myself of important tasks. For ease of reference, the tasks are organized by the person responsible; responsibility category—management, curriculum/instruction, assessment, staff, student/parent; and within each category as "ongoing," "fall, "winter," and "spring."

(Text continues on page 154.)

Figure 6.3. Principal Daily Checklist

	MON	TUE	WED	THUR	FRI
STUDENT SERVICES MEETING					
STAFF MEETING					
INTERVENTION TEAM MEETING					
CALENDAR					
TICKLER FILE					
SECRETARY CONTACT					
ASSISTANT CONTACT					
VOICE MAIL					
E-MAILS					
SNAIL MAIL					
CLASSROOM VISITS					
TEACHER OBSERVATIONS					
DISCIPLINE					
PARENT DISCIPLINE CALLS					
RETURN PHONE CALLS					
COPYING					
BOARD AND OTHER REPORTS					
PRIORITY PROJECTS					

GOALS & ACTIVITIES	
Mon.	
Tue.	
Wed.	
Thur.	
Fri.	

Figure 6.4. Major Assignments

	Management	Teaching & Learning	Assessment	Staff	Students & Parents	Other
Principal	**Ongoing:** Budget Ordering Emergency drills Food service/custodial Weekly bulletins E-mail newsbreaks Parent newsletters **Fall:** Emergency handbook Emergency protocols Emergency forms Check-in packet Open house **Spring:** Check-out packet	Improvement plan Curriculum maps Math curriculum Science alignment Band/music Highly Capable program Leadership Academy	Interim assessments Reading Comprehension State Assessments	Staff meetings Staff handbook Teacher observations Goal conferences Goal plans Observations Disciplinary actions Book studies First aid training Staff advisory	Discipline Bus referrals Talented Tigers K-3 Principal lunch 4–5 Reward movies Gr. 4–5 awards Gr. 5 graduation Parent handbook Parent meetings/events Choir & band Concerts K orientation K graduations P-T conferences Child Protective Services liaison Student Services Team	Admin. agreement Board reports Leadership academy reports Gr. 5 recess & lunch Supervision Student pickup supervision

	Management	Teaching & Learning	Assessment	Staff	Students & Parents	Other
Assistant	Emergency prep. Sub handbooks Trimester plan Schedules Bus dismissal	Open court Imagine it FOSS WSLA Writing nonnegotiables	Fluency 2-Minute write 3-Minute math State testing Report cards Highly Capable eligibility	Teacher coach Classified evals Open Ct. training Imagine It training Science training Teacher Assistance program	Discipline Discipline plan Behavior room Intervention Team Attendance Shuttle bus approval Student placement K-12 parent handbook Hi-Cap student plans P-T conferences Success in education Veterans' Day assembly Volunteer lunch	Attendance reports Weapons reports

Is the school leader's life hopeless? Not if you keep on top of your workload. If things are a getting out of control in your office, take time to identify priority goals, responsibilities, and daily priorities. Your load will seem lighter and your work life a lot less chaotic.

Keep Organized

It was a naval officer who inspired me to keep organized. He had dropped by my office in late June to learn about my school. Fortunately, I had just finished tidying up, a dreaded chore that was tackled at the close of each school year because by then my workspace was a complete mess. This year there had been stacks of paperwork to be filed, manila folders stuffed to the gills to be weeded and replaced in file cabinets, reference books to be shelved, and my collection of stuffed toys, building blocks, and picture books to be sorted out. But now, after a couple days of work, my desk was clear of document debris, the bookshelf dusted and reorganized, papers neatly filed away, and kid toys attractively arranged on their shelves.

The officer was newly posted to a nearby naval base after months at sea and he was shopping around for a school for his young children. He spent an hour quizzing me about my philosophy of education, the school's mission, our state assessment results, and how our discipline system worked. When he departed he said that this school was definitely the one for his children. I wondered what had most influenced his decision—our rising test scores, the clarity of our school mission, or the nurturing nature of our discipline program? Curious, I asked what helped him to make up his mind. "It's this office," he replied, taking in the orderly shelves, neat desktop, and artfully arranged toys. "Everything is neatly stowed away—a sign of good management. On a ship, having everything organized and in its proper place is essential to a smooth and safe operation. I can tell this school runs well."

From that day forward I made an effort to keep things orderly—not just at the close of the year but on a day-to-day basis. This effort not only improved the appearance of my office but also my efficiency. This, in turn, lowered my stress because my uncluttered environment was restful to the eyes and essential documents and files were at my fingertips.

I improved my organizational skills by talking to colleagues and reading books about the subject, such as Frank Buck's superb guide *Get Organized*! (2008). I use a dozen or more organizational tools now but these are my top ten:

- *Conference Notebook:* I keep my conference notes from meetings with students, staff, and parents in *one* three-ring binder filled with lined notebook paper, divided by the month. Each entry is dated and the name of the person I am meeting with heads each notation. I like having just one binder to work with—I tried separate notebooks for students, staff, and clients but was always searching for the right one. The monthly dividers are helpful because if I have to review notes, I can usually recall the month the conference took place. This notebook is archived at the end of each school year in case I need to refer to the entries again. This might seem unlikely but sometimes you are asked for information that goes back years, such as with a lawsuit, a parental custody dispute, or Child Protective Services review.

- *Planner:* A good planner is not just a tool for recording meetings and events; use it to keep track of major responsibilities, personal goal activities, and tasks associated with your school improvement plan. Over the years I have used electronic planners as well as "hard copy" versions and either works fine. Whichever you prefer, make sure your planner is kept up to date and that you keep it with you. That way you can check your calendar, schedule meetings, or enter planning notes wherever you are.
- *School Bulletin Binder:* I keep everything I need to write the weekly bulletin in a three-ring binder. Included are the school and district calendars; school schedules—daily, specialist, staff KP duty, display case; staff birthdays; and the trimester plan, which provides dates for academic screenings, state assessments, and report card distribution. There are also reference documents that I add on a short-term basis, such as bulletins and emails from staff members that I save if I will need to refer to them when writing a future bulletin.
- *A–Z Files:* I file everything from A to Z in cabinets by these categories: School Operation & Management, Personnel, Curriculum & Instruction, State Assessments, School Screenings & Assessments, Student Guidance & Services, and Archived Files. Each category has its own file drawer so items are easy to find.
- *Tickler Files:* I have a small crate that sits on my back counter where I can file documents that I will need later by the month and date. I check this daily to retrieve items that I need that day, such as a meeting agenda, personnel write up, or a teacher evaluation report.

- *In–Active–Out Stacking Tray:* I have a three-tier stacking tray that sits on a corner of my desk. The top compartment is labeled IN and holds incoming mail and other documents routed to me; the second compartment—labeled ACTIVE—holds project files in current use; and the bottom tier, labeled OUT, has outgoing mail, documents, and files to be "processed." By "processed" I mean filed, distributed, or returned to a staff member via district courier.
- *Frequently Used Items:* There are some items that I definitely need at my finger tips and I keep these in stacking trays on a counter adjacent to my desk. These include frequently used forms, such as those needed for Copy Center requests, teacher observations, and staff and student Good News notes; log in notebooks—police contacts, 911 calls, Child Protective Services referrals; and references, such as student No Contact orders, demographic updates, and medical emergency lists. I can quickly grab what I need at a moment's notice.
- *Budget Binder:* This notebook is divided into budget categories, such as building, library, staff development, and various grants. I log-in approved expenditures and keep a running total on an Excel spreadsheet. That way I always know how much money I have to work with in any category and can compare my figures to the fiscal reports I get from the district. The notebook also includes all the pertinent budget codes, copies of required forms, and fiscal bulletins from the business office.
- *Discipline Reference Guide:* This includes copies of the district discipline guide, the discipline matrix for the elementary level, our school discipline handbook, procedures for disciplinary action, and samples of required forms. Discipline records are kept on our school database that is kept up by a school secretary. When I am dealing with a case, it is easier to access the database than it is to search for discipline writeups.
- *Supervision & Evaluation Notebook:* Expectations, such as the state professional code of conduct and our school norms, are placed in this notebook. Included are the names of the teachers and specialists I evaluate; their contract status, such as leave replacement, provisional, continuing; supervision and evaluation procedures; copies of needed forms; and a place to record observation and progress conference dates.

Keeping things organized and easy to access has made my job easier. As a bonus, my staff and clients say visiting my orderly office is always a pleasure.

Suggested Readings

Buck, Frank. (2008). *Get organized! Time management for school leaders.* Larchmont, NY: Eye on Education.

Simon, Richard A., & Newman, James F. (2004). *Making time to lead: How principals can stay on top of it all.* Thousand Oaks, CA: Corwin Press.

Perfect Performance

School leaders are expected to be excellent instructional leaders and at the same time, astute organizational managers. Engineering academic success coupled with the day-to-day challenges of running a school, however, is stressful for even the most well-prepared and experienced administrator. The difficulties are substantial and include:

- Children and adolescents requiring specialized instruction and long-term support: English language learners, medically fragile children, students with learning difficulties or behavior disorders, homeless youngsters, and students from impoverished families.
- Teachers who require skilled supervision: beginning teachers whose talents are just emerging, experienced teachers whose enthusiasm for their mission needs a jumpstart, and ineffectual teachers who require continuous monitoring.
- Instability within the profession: shifting curriculum trends, contradictory research regarding instructional best practice, and ever-changing state and federal accountability requirements.
- Management challenges: mushrooming regulations governing health, nutrition, safety, communications, personnel, and security; contentious classified and certificated unions; parent pressure groups—from special education to gifted education; and rising costs but shoestring budgets.

These job demands—and the pressures that accompany them—require school leaders to be top performers.

How can principals perfect performance? By mastering the knowledge, values, and skills outlined in professional standards. These can be found in *Leading Learning Communities: What Principals Should Know and*

Be Able to Do (NAESP, 2008). This newly updated sourcebook identifies six ambitious standards covering student and adult learning, diverse communities, twenty-first century career demands, performance based accountability, data analysis, and parent and community engagement. *Leading Learning Communities* helps new and veteran principals sharpen their leadership skills.

Principals also perfect performance by learning from the successes and failures of their day-to-day leadership experiences, completing professional development coursework, and reading professional books and journals. Although independent learning is valuable, it is not as powerful as collaborative learning. This comes about when administrative colleagues form learning teams. What are learning teams? Nothing more than "groups of professionals who—both together and through a collaborative process—increase results, knowledge, and competence within the group by contributing their individual experiences, insights, and skills to the group" (West & Derrington, 2009, p. 77).

Here are five powerful strategies for administrators striving to become an effective learning team (West, 2011):

- ♦ Initiate book studies—explore leadership concepts, such as the school improvement ideas presented in *10 Traits of Highly Effective Schools: Raising the Achievement Bar for All Students* (McEwan, 2009) or the team-building strategies covered in *Leadership Teaming: The Superintendent-Principal Relationship* (West & Derrington, 2009).
- ♦ Share stories about successful efforts to improve teacher performance, increase student achievement, or strengthen parent participation.
- ♦ Make time at administrative meetings to discuss, debate, and apply promising ideas gleaned from professional journals, such as *Education Leadership*, *Phi Delta Kappan*, and *Principal*.
- ♦ Schedule team members to share their school improvement efforts, leadership techniques, and organizational tools, such as achievement data analysis software.
- ♦ Participate in professional conferences as a group and collaboratively decide how to best use new information to enhance teacher and student performance.
- ♦ Be credible instructional leaders—participate in the *same* inservice activities as your teachers. Figure 6.5, which outlines the staff development my teachers need, serves as a quick guide.

Figure 6.5. Staff Development Guide

Curriculum & Instruction	Health, Safety, Legal Issues	Other
Math Core math program Computational fluency testing State math standards	**Student Health** Drug-alcohol prevention Core health program	**Staff Relationships** Code of ethics & collaboration
Reading Core reading program Reading incentive program Oral reading fluency Schoolwide assessments	**Emergency Procedures** Emergency handbook Emergency protocols Code Blue Team Restraint procedures	**Student Discipline** Discipline handbook Behavior interventions Behavior referrals Bus citations Choices program Alternative placement IEP & 504 students
Writing Process writing Writing prompts Schoolwide assessments	**First Aid Response** Epi-pens Diabetes Seizures Defibrillator Basic first aid	**Student Support** Intervention Team Student Study Team Counselor services Behavior room access
Science Core science program Supplemental science programs	**School Security** Alarm system Online emergency website School security procedures	**Policies** Harassment & intimidation Violence, threats FERPA Affirmative action, equity Student records Drug, tobacco, gun free Whistleblower
Social Studies Core social studies program Classroom-based assessments	**Legal Issues** Copyright law Custody issues Teacher liability Federal, state, district policies	**Computers** E-mail system & policies School database Internet use policies Equipment & software Online resources

(Figure continues on next page.)

Models & Expectations State standards: all subjects Response to intervention (RTI) Differentiated instruction K-12 reading model		**Agencies & Services** Child Protective Services Homeless students Special education 504 Students
Assessments Oral reading fluency Computational fluency State assessments Progress monitoring		**School Improvement** Goal setting Progress reviews Data collection & analysis Professional learning communities

Ongoing professional development takes time and effort but the payoff is invaluable. Stronger skills make school leadership easier, less stressful, and more rewarding.

Suggested Readings

Association for Supervision and Curriculum Development. *Educational Leadership*. www.ascd.org

Phi Delta Kappa International. *Phi Delta Kappan*. www.pdkintl.org

National Association of Elementary School Principals. *Principal*. www.naesp.org

Summing Up

- Manage stress to avoid serious health problems and professional dysfunction.
- Keep stress generators under control by creating stress-response plans.
- Stay physically fit and emotionally healthy.
- Set goals that build on previous work, align with district initiatives, and are achievable.
- Control your workload.
- Perfect performance through professional development.

Making Connections

- What are your stress symptoms? Make a list of the physical and emotional indicators. How do you respond to stress? If your response isn't working for you, what would you like to do differently?
- What steps have you taken to control your workload and keep organized? Contact colleagues to learn their organizational tricks.

Strengthening Professional Practice

- Craft a personal wellness plan that includes ways to stay physically fit and emotionally healthy. Include a daily/weekly activity schedule and a timeline for implementation.
- Are you a top-flight administrator? What areas do you need to perfect? Review the professional standards in *Leading Learning Communities* then create a professional development plan that includes self-reflection, individual study, and collective learning.

Conclusion

Life is not a matter of holding good cards, but sometimes, playing a poor hand well.

— Jack London (1876–1916)

In the fourteenth century, an insightful theory was crafted by a Franciscan monk named William of Ockham (also known as Occam; spelling was a bit dicey in the fourteenth century). Ockham posited that in regards to most things—observable phenomena, historical events, societal situations, and imponderable problems—simplicity trumps complexity. In other words, the simplest explanation or solution is usually the most sensible one. Ockham's theory, which came to be known as Occam's Razor (the word *razor* referring to the shaving away of extraneous information or variables), has been successfully applied—from the fourteenth century to the present—to the fields of philosophy, science, medicine, biology, religion, and mathematics (Wikipedia, 2010).

It was in the spirit of William of Ockham that I wrote *Problem-Solving Tools and Tips for School Leaders.* Simple, easy-to-implement solutions are often the best way to tackle complex, perplexing problems. The "simple-is-better" approach is also the one I took in preparing these concluding remarks. I surmised that busy school leaders would appreciate the succinctness of the theme and chapter summaries that follow:

Theme I: Perfecting Problem-Solving Performance

- Be proactive—strive to prevent problems through thoughtful planning and preparation.
- Tackle problems quickly, intentionally, optimistically, and proficiently.
- Stay constructive and grow from setbacks.

Theme 2: Counteracting Workplace Negativity

- Look for signs of workplace negativity and take necessary action.
- Engage your staff members in constructive behaviors.
- Model and actively nurture a culture of positiveness.

Theme 3: Stopping Staff Misconduct

- Prevent employee misconduct by setting expectations, communicating responsibilities, and providing sufficient training.
- Intervene when staff misconduct arises.
- Nurture professional behavior through example, in-service, and coaching.

Theme 4: Mastering Emergency Management

- Plan ahead so that you can confidently handle any emergency.
- Practice emergency response actions with staff and students.
- Manage emergencies more effectively by activating a support team.

Theme 5: Breaking Through Success Barriers

- Bring coherence to your school's efforts to improve student learning.
- Create a theory of action and strategies to bring about effective change.
- Be results oriented—use sound data to judge the effectiveness of your actions.

Theme 6: Derailing Leadership Distress

- Recognize and take control of stress producers.
- Engage in activities that enhance your physical and emotional wellbeing.
- Manage responsibilities realistically and efficiently.

I hope *Problem-Solving Tools and Tips for School Leaders* offered new strategies to add to your leadership toolkit and provided resources that will help you prevent problems from materializing in your school. As a final note, keep in mind that it was the wise counsel that I received from other educators that gave me the idea for this book. I still reach out for support—don't hesitate to do the same.

Cathie E. West
cathiewest@comcast.net

Additional Suggested Readings

The following books present concepts and skills that will help school leaders become professionally proficient problem solvers:

Culver, Mary. (2009). *Applying servant leadership in today's schools*. Larchmont, NY: Eye On Education.

Edmonson, Stacey, Combs, Julie, & Harris, Sandra. (2008). *Managing conflict*. Larchmont, NY: Eye On Education.

Fleck, Franzy. (2005). *What successful principals do!* Larchmont, NY: Eye On Education.

Fullan, Michael. (2005). *Leadership & sustainability: Systems thinkers in action*. Thousand Oaks, CA: Corwin Press.

Goleman, Daniel. (2006). *Social intelligence: The revolutionary new science of human relationships*. New York, NY: Bantam Dell.

Lindle, Jane Clark. (2005). *20 School strategies for collaborative school leaders*. Larchmont, NY: Eye On Education.

Marzano, Robert J., Waters, Timothy, & McNulty, Brian A. (2005). *School leadership that works: From research to results*. Aurora, CO: Mid-continent Research for Education and Learning.

Sagor, Richard. (2005). *The action research guidebook: A four-step process for educators and school teams*. Thousand Oaks, CA: Corwin Press.

Salzar, Pamela S. (2008). *High-impact leadership for high-impact schools*. Larchmont, NY: Eye On Education.

Sparks, Dennis. (2005). *Leading for results: Transforming teaching, learning, and relationships in schools*. Thousand Oaks, CA: Corwin Press.

References

Anonymous. (2009). Japanese Proverb: *Fix the problem, not the blame.* Retrieved December 3, 2009 from http://www.quoteland.com/author.asp.

Beatty, C. A., & Barker Scott, B. A. (2004). *Building smart teams: Roadmap to high performance.* Thousand Oaks, CA: Sage Publications.

Buck, F. (2008). *Get organized! Time management for school leaders.* Larchmont, NY: Eye On Education.

Center for Education & Employment Law. (2009). *Keeping your school safe & secure: A practical guide.* Third edition. Malvern, PA: Author.

City, E. A., Elmore, R. F., Fiarman, S. E., & Teitel, L. (2009). *Instructional rounds in education: A network approach to improving teaching and learning.* Cambridge, MA: Harvard Education Press.

Copland, M. A., & Knapp, M. S. (2006). *Connecting leadership with learning: A framework for reflection, planning, and action.* Alexandra, VA: Association for Supervision and Curriculum Development.

Copland, M. A. (2009). *The cycle of inquiry: A process for leading improvement in teaching and learning.* Retrieved June 1, 2010 from http:wsla.psesd.org/pressroom/articles/cycle_of _inquiry_09.php.

Dolan, W. P. (1994). *Restructuring our schools: A primer on systematic change.* Kansas City, MO: Systems & Organizations.

Federal Emergency Management Agency. (2009). *Introduction to incident command system, ICS-100.* Retrieved June 21, 2010 from http://training.fema.gov/EMIWeb/IS/IS100a.asp.

Foxman, P. (2007). *Dancing with fear: Controlling stress and creating a life beyond panic and anxiety.* Second edition. Alameda, CA: Hunter House.

Fullan, M. (2005). *Leadership and sustainability: System thinkers in action.* Thousand Oaks, CA: Corwin Press.

Fullan, M. (2008). *The six secrets of change: What the best leaders do to help their organizations to survive and thrive.* San Francisco: CA: John Wiley & Sons.

Get Smart. (2004). Vol 6. Miami, FL: ARISE Foundation.

Ginsberg, R. (2008). Being boss is hard: The emotional side of being in charge. *Phi Delta Kappan: The Journal for Education, 90*(4), 292–297.

Goleman, D. (2006). *Social intelligence: The revolutionary new science of human relationships.* New York, NY: Bantam Books.

Granite Falls School District #322. (2010). *Strategic plan*. Unpublished document.

Harwayne, S. (1999). *Going public: Priorities and practice at the Manhattan New School*. Portsmouth, NH: Heinemann.

Heathfield, S. M. (2009). *Tips for minimizing workplace negativity: Managing and solving workplace negativity*. Retrieved December 20, 2009 from http://humanresources.about.com/od/workrelationships/a/negativity.htm.

Johnson, S. (1709–1784). Quote: *Your manuscript is both good and original, but the part that is good is not original and the part that is original is not good*. Retrieved June 25, 2010 from http://www.quotationspage.com/quote/23678.html.

Lawrence, C. E., & Vachon, M. K. (2003). *How to handle staff misconduct*. Second edition. Thousand Oaks, CA: Corwin Press.

London, J. (1876–1916). Quote: *Life is not a matter of holding good cards, but sometimes, playing a poor hand well*. Retrieved June 23, 2010 from http://quotationsbook.com/quote/6810.

Lopper, J. (2008). *How to counteract negativity in the workplace: Overcome a Negative work environment with a positive attitude*. Retrieved December 20, 2009 from http://www.suite101.com/content/how-to-counteract-negativity-in-the-workplace-a82156.

MacKenzie, R. J. (2006). *Setting limits in the classroom: How to move beyond the dance of discipline in today's classrooms*. New York, NY: Three Rivers Press.

McEwan, E. K. (2002). *10 Traits of highly effective teachers: How to hire, coach, and mentor successful teachers*. Thousand Oaks, CA: Corwin Press.

McEwan, E. K. (2005). *How to deal with teachers who are angry, troubled, exhausted, or just plain confused*. Thousand Oaks, CA: Corwin Press.

McEwan, E. K. (2009). *10 Traits of highly effective schools: Raising the achievement bar for all students*. Thousand Oaks, CA: Corwin Press.

National Association of Elementary School Principals. (2008). *Leading Learning Communities: Standards for what principals should know and be able to do*. Alexandria, VA: Author.

Nyland, L. (2008) *Mathematics: Finding what works-a personal quest*. Retrieved June 15, 2010 from http://www.wasaoly.org/Content/NavigationMenu/ABOUTWASA/News/WhitePapers/ Mathematics0708.pdf.

Office of the Superintendent of Public Instruction (Washington), 2005. *School improvement planning: Process guide*. Retrieved December 26, 2009 from http://www.k12.wa.us/SchoolImprovement/Guide.aspx.

Paine, T. (1776). Quote: *I love the man that can smile in trouble, that can gather strength from distress and grow brave by reflection.* Retrieved August 16, 2009 from http://www.quoteland.com/search.asp.

Queen, J. A., & Queen, P. S. (2005). *The frazzled principal's wellness plan: Reclaiming time, managing stress, and creating a healthy life style.* Thousand Oaks, CA: Corwin Press.

Shannon, G. S., & Bylsma, P. (2007). *The nine characteristics of high-performing schools: A research-based resource for schools and districts to assist with improving student learning.* Second edition. Retrieved December 25, 2009 from http://www.k12.wa.us.edu/research/pubdocs/NineCharacteristics.pdf.

Thomas, S. J. (2004). *Using web and paper questionnaires for data-based decision making: From design to interpretation of results.* Thousand Oaks, CA: Corwin Press.

Vaill, A. (1998). *Everybody was so young: Gerald and Sara Murphy: A lost generation love story.* New York, NY: Broadway Books.

Wayne, J. (1907–1979) Quote: *Courage is being scared to death—but saddling up anyway.* Retrieved February 7, 2010 from http://www.quotationspage.com/quote/2111.html.

Wells, H. G. (1866–1946). Quote: *No passion in the world is equal to the passion to alter someone else's draft.* Retrieved June 25, 2010 from http://www.quotationspage.com/quote/5117.html

West, C. E. (1995, January). How to perk up the dreaded staff meeting. *Principal, 74,* 47–48.

West, C. E. (1997, September). Writing weekly bulletins for teachers. *Principal, 77,* 51–52.

West, C. E. (2011, January/February). School leadership teaming. *Principal, 90,* 10–13.

West, C. E., & Derrington, M. L. (2009). *Leadership teaming: The superintendent-principal relationship.* Thousand Oaks, CA: Corwin Press.

Whittaker, T., & Zoul, J. (2008). *The 4 core factors for school success.* Larchmont, NY: Eye On Education.

Wikipedia. *Occam's razor.* Retrieved June 23, 2010 from http://en.wikipedia.org/wiki/Occam%27s_razor.